UNIQUE
AND
UNUSUAL
PLACES
IN THE
MID-
ATLANTIC
REGION

William N. Hoffman

SPRING GARDEN PUBLICATIONS CO.
P.O. Box 7131
Lancaster, PA 17604-7131

UNIQUE and UNUSUAL PLACES
in the MID-ATLANTIC REGION

Published by:
Spring Garden Publications Co.
P.O. Box 7131-B
Lancaster, Pennsylvania 17604-7131

Printed and bound in the United States of America

ISBN: 0-9612050-6-7

First edition: June, 1995

TABLE OF CONTENTS

TABLE OF CONTENTS (continued)

TABLE OF CONTENTS (continued)

PENNSYLVANIA (continued)

TABLE OF CONTENTS (continued)

PENNSYLVANIA (continued)

Bold type identifies discount coupon advertiser. See page 157.

6

INTRODUCTION

The Mid-Atlantic Region is filled with all kinds of museums, historic sites, scenic areas, and outstanding man-made structure. Some are justly renowned, many largely unknown.

This book presents the one- or few-of-a-kind places that are too often overlooked. It's not because they're unworthy of attention, but because they're small and lack the funds necessary to do the advertising to get noticed.

This book is not "ghost-written" from promotional literature supplied by the museums or by site managers. I physically visited virtually all the places you'll be reading about, missing only a few that are seasonal.

How were the sites selected? The dictionary defines "unique" as "one and only, single, sole, different from all others;" "unusual" means "not usual or common, rare, exceptional." Those definitions guided my selections. The adjective "unique" is very precise: something is unique, or it isn't. The term "unusual" is much more subjective. Here I relied on my perspective as a travel writer and traveler.

There are a few famous sites in this book; they're here because they're unique. After all, a location's fame should not be a reason to exclude it. But in order to keep the book to manageable size, and to highlight the lesser-known places, I established further criteria for inclusion. I eliminated certain types of places that are relatively common: art museums; historic homes and buildings (unless they have some other unusual significance attached to them); museums commemorating historical events; children's museums; antique car museums; local history museums; natural areas that, despite having great scenic value, are not otherwise unique; and, similiarly, landmark structures. A particular auto museum, for example, may have the world's largest collection of Duesenbergs, but that in itself does not make it unique or unusual, because auto museums are not rare. But the world's only museum devoted to, say, the display of foreign license plates, is definitely unique, and therefore would qualify for this book.

The majority of Unique and Unusual Places are museums, but I was careful not to overlook unique and unusual natural areas and man-made structures that many travelers ignore. The Mid-Atlantic region has an immensely diverse geography and an equally diverse history of development by peoples of many nationalities. The legacies of man and nature are also captured here.

A unique or unusual place is not automatically created by moving the contents of someone's attic into a storefront, calling it a museum, and charging admission. There has to be a recognizable theme (or themes) that's portrayed clearly and in reasonably organized fashion by the displays. If there is, then it's a true museum, and it became a candidate for this book.

Many unusual museums have been developed in small towns by local people who saw a value in preserving and displaying an outstanding collection of whatever that happened to be located in their community. These folks had no government grants or large endowments for museum development, but their enthusiasm and dedication are boundless. Whether or not their displays are world-class, if they had something unique or unusual to show and had made at least a start at presenting it in a coherent manner, it's here.

You may know of a place that you believe should have been included. Chances are I did consider it; I visited many more than the 126 sites actually chosen, but there's always the possibility that I failed to uncover a few in my research. Please feel free to write with your recommendations, or, for that matter, any other comments you have about this book. I'll gladly consider your suggestions for future editions. All letters will be answered—guaranteed!

Although I've made some editorial comments about the sites, the book is primarily an information source. However, the very fact that these sites are included is a *de facto* recommendation that they're worth visiting. You may not be interested in visiting every location, but by giving you the full range of Unique and Unusual Places, you'll be able to make your own choices.

A few words about the "nuts and bolts" information accompanying each listing. **Address** is the street address; the zip code (zip) is for the town under which the entry appears. If the mailing address is different from the street address, it is given. **Hours of operation** and **admission** charges were correct at press time, but please verify with a phone call to make sure there haven't been major changes, especially if several years have passed before you get around to visiting. **Handicapped access** refers to wheelchair accessibility, and may or may not apply to persons using other kinds of mobility aids. **Time needed** is my estimate of how long you should allow for a thorough tour, whether escorted or self-guided. Your actual time could be more or less, depending on your interest. **Location** is a more precise description than the map accompanying most listings (where needed) can provide. The only other map you will need is a state road map to get you to the city or town in question.

Directional signs to many museums have been posted along major highways, but the signs occasionally are missing or damaged. In Philadelphia and Washington, where parking is limited and expensive, I recommend walking and/or public transportation to travel between sites.

Enjoy the many Unique and Unusual Places in the Mid-Atlantic Region!

DELAWARE

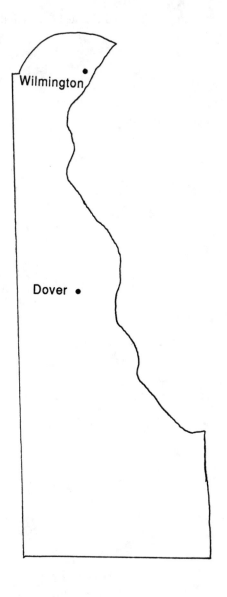

Dover (Kent County)

Johnson Victrola Museum

Address: Bank Lane & New Street (zip 19901)
Phone: (302) 739-3262
Hours: Tuesday-Saturday except holidays 10 to
3:30
Admission: free; donations accepted
Handicapped access: fully accessible
Parking: Free parking lot on premises, free street
parking available

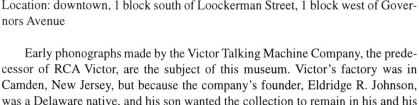

Time needed: 30-45 minutes
Location: downtown, 1 block south of Loockerman Street, 1 block west of Governors Avenue

Early phonographs made by the Victor Talking Machine Company, the predecessor of RCA Victor, are the subject of this museum. Victor's factory was in Camden, New Jersey, but because the company's founder, Eldridge R. Johnson, was a Delaware native, and his son wanted the collection to remain in his and his father's home state, the museum was established in Dover in 1967.

The development of Victrola technology is shown in the table and floor model machines on display. Features such as pre-set automatic stops, electric pickups, and spring-wound motors gradually made record-playing more convenient and improved the sound quality. In addition to several dozen players dating from the company's earliest days (it was founded in 1901) until the development of electrically operated machines, there is a large collection of 78-rpm records, for which Victor was also famous. Records are played on several of the machines during the course of the guided tour. Photos of some of the famous Victor recording artists line the walls.

Although Victor talking machines have long since passed into history, the museum is still adding to its collection as significant pieces become available. You can even buy replacement needles for your own Victrola in the museum's gift shop.

11

Wilmington (New Castle County)

Delaware Toy and Miniature Museum

Address: SR 141 (mail: PO Box
4053, Wilmington 19807)
Phone: (302) 427-TOYS (8697)
Hours: Tuesday-Saturday 10 to 4,
Sunday noon to 5
Admission:
Handicapped access: ground floor
only
Parking: free parking lot on premises
Time needed: about 1 hour
Location: just north of Wilmington.
Museum is 2.2 miles west of US 202
and 0.1 miles east of SR 100. En-
trance driveway shared with Hagley
Museum.

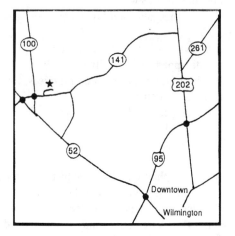

A new museum (opened October 7, 1994) housing the extensive dollhouse and toy collection of founders Gloria Hinkel and Beverly Thomes (mother and daughter). It's located in a building that has seen service as the boiler house for the adjacent Hagley Museum as well as a records storage center for the DuPont Corporation, headquartered in Wilmington. The collection occupies two rooms and a hallway on the ground floor and two rooms upstairs. The museum owns most of the items on display, but there are also changing traveling exhibits.

Each dollhouse is exquisitely decorated and furnished in great detail with period pieces—tables, chairs, rugs, even wallpaper. The museum's showpiece is an 1895 dollhouse made by the English firm Lines Co. It has electricity and a water tank in the attic from which the bathtub and kitchen sink can be filled.

There are also several antique kitchens that were used as children's teaching tools, miniature furniture made by craftsmen as sales pieces to show their skills to prospective customers, a model of a still-standing 1860 house in the Germantown section of Philadelphia, and a working 1875 musical French opera house. There's also a working 1890 steam plant that powers mechanical toys.

Among the assortment of toys and games are miniature card games, tin windup banks, early 1900s steam-powered toys, old erector sets, HO and Lionel gauge trains, dolls and furnishings from the mid-19th century, and 1940s vintage plastic furniture.

The second floor houses the newer pieces (Victorian era to about 1950), including a reproduction of the dining room in the home of Mrs. Jean Austin DuPont with its sterling silver placesettings, pettipoint run, and chair cushions, a working 1910 Empire electric stove, beer steins, and 1920s tinware, all in miniature. There is a fully furnished 8-room English Tudor house.

Almost all items on display are identified as to date and origin, in case you're looking around on your own. If your visit gets you hooked on these incredibly detailed "historic playthings", you can start your own collection in the museum's gift shop. There is also a library upstairs should you wish to research anything you buy or have in your own attic.

13

DISTRICT OF COLUMBIA

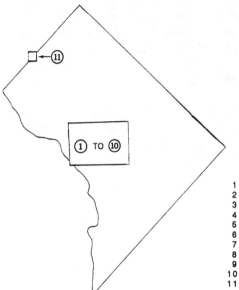

1 B'nai B'rith Klutznick National Jewish Museum
2 Bureau of Engraving and Printing
3 Federal Bureau of Investigation
4 The Holography Collection
5 National Building Museum
6 National Museum of American Jewish Military History
7 National Postal Museum
8 Textile Museum
9 U.S. Department of the Interior Museum
10 U.S. Holocaust Memorial Museum
11 Washington Dolls' House and Toy Museum

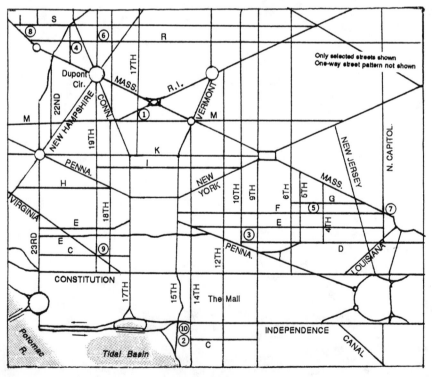

B'nai B'rith Klutznick National Jewish Museum

Address: 1640 Rhode Island Avenue, NW (zip 20036)
Phone: (202) 857-6583
Hours: Sunday-Friday 10 to 5 except federal and Jewish holidays
Admission: free; donations accepted
Handicapped access: fully accessible
Parking: metered street parking, but spaces often limited
Time needed: about 1 hour
Location: southeast corner of 17th Street and Rhode Island Avenue. Metro (Red Line) to Farragut North (Connecticut Ave. & K or L Sts.); walk east on K or L to 17th, north on 17th to Rhode Island (between M and N).

Founded in 1843, B'nai B'rith is the oldest Jewish service organization in the United States and the largest in the world. The museum was established in 1957 and is named for Philip Klutznick, a Chicago attorney who also served in the administrations of Presidents Franklin Roosevelt, Kennedy, and Carter. It contains very informative and instructive displays of Jewish life items and observances.

The permanent exhibits are "The Life Cycle" and Sabbath and holiday exhibits. All three explain well the major milestones in a Jew's life and the meaning and importance of the Sabbath and holidays. Ritual items connected with these observances are on view, and include metal stamps used to identify Kosher meat; Kiddush cups; 17th century Sabbath candlesticks from Danzig, Poland; a set of 3rd century B.C. incantation bowls; and a miniature Bible used by traveling rabbis. Ceremonial objects as well as cards, books, and other Judaica are sold in the gift shop.

Among the museum's most prized possessions are letters written in 1790 between George Washington and Moses Seixas, sexton of the famous Touro synagogue in Newport, Rhode Island, one of the nation's oldest. Washington's letter contains the oft-quoted phrase "to bigotry no sanction, to persecution no assistance", used by various religious and ethnic groups to promote tolerance.

Recent additions to the museum have included the Jewish American Sports Hall of Fame and a gallery for works of major Jewish artists of the past 150 years. A sculpture garden to the rear of the museum features works by Philip Ratner.

Changing exhibits are shown in the entry gallery; recent offerings have included "Ethiopian Jewish Life 1983-1992", "Jewish Threads in the Muslim Moroccan Tapestry", and "How and What Does a Jew Growing Up in Germany After the Holocaust, Paint?"

Bureau of Engraving and Printing

Address: 14th and C Streets, SW (zip 20228) (map page 14)
Phone: (202) 874-3019
Hours: Monday-Friday 9 to 2 except federal holidays
Admission: free
Handicapped access: entry foyer and gift shop only
Parking: metered street parking, some free but timed parking on The Mall. Spaces often limited.
Time needed: 1/2 hour
Location: west side of 14th Street opposite C Street. Metro (Blue and Orange Lines) to Smithsonian (12th & Independence Ave.), walk west on Independence to 14th, left 1 block to C.

This is the only place in the country where paper currency is printed (stamps are also printed here). After a 5-minute introductory film portraying the history of the Bureau, visitors are taken on a guided 20-minute tour where they see three stages in the 65-step process of currency production. The tour is rather hurried, although you will have the chance to ask questions of the guide.

First is the manual engraving process, known as intaglio printing, which produces the master die from which bills and stamps are printed (stamp production is not part of the tour). The next stop is at examining and trimming, where rejects are shredded and sold in the Visitors Center in the basement of the building. Sorry, no free samples. Finally, at overprinting and packaging, the serial number, Treasury seal, and Federal Reserve Bank codes are added to make the bills legal tender. Guillotine cutters cut the sheets of 32 bills into single stacks of 100 bills which are packaged for shipment to the twelve Federal Reserve banks.

Before or after the tour, you can view the exhibit in the entry hall of the history of money (paper, especially). The Visitors Center has display cases showing the merchandise sold there. To buy anything, obtain an order form and mark your choices before going to the sales window. Items sold include mint coins, uncut currency, small portraits of all Presidents (through Bush), large portraits of Washington, Jefferson, Lincoln, Grant, and all Presidents from McKinley through Bush, and photographs of important Washington public landmarks.

Federal Bureau of Investigation

Address: 10th Street and Pennsylvania Avenue, NW (zip 20535) (map page 14)
Phone: (202) 324-3447
Hours: Monday-Friday 9 to 4:15 except federal holidays

Admission: free
Handicapped access: entry foyer only
Parking: metered street parking or public garages
Time needed: 1 hour plus waiting time
Location: tour entrance on south side of E Street between 9th and 10th. Metro (Yellow Line) to Archives (7th & Pennsylvania), walk west on Pennsylvania to 9th, right on 9th to E, left 1/2 block on E; or Red, Blue, and Orange Lines to Metro Center (12th & G Sts.), walk south on 12th to E, left 2-1/2 blocks on E.

All visitors must pass through security clearance, and cameras are not permitted. The one-hour tour includes three parts of the Bureau: exhibits, the crime lab, and a live firearms demonstration.

The exhibit area on the main level includes photos of the 8 most wanted criminals in the Bureau's history (John Dillinger, Baby Face Nelson, Bonnie Parker, et. al.), the current top 10 most wanted, and pictorial displays on the National Crime Information Center, illicit drugs, organized crime, terrorism, violent crime, and the FBI memorial honoring agents killed on duty.

The tour then proceeds to the second level, where visitors view a firearms reference collection, memorabilia formerly used in the FBI's lab, the materials analysis unit, where items obtained during the normal course of work are analyzed to determine what they are and what they were used for, microscopic analysis, the firearms and tool marking unit, a display window of forfeitures—items seized in drug raids, and the potentially most interesting part, the DNA analysis. The latter is a working lab, so anything could be undergoing inspection as the tour passes.

The firearms demonstration, which sometimes requires a wait until two or more tour groups are combined, is conducted by an agent using a .38, a repeating pistol, and a Tommy gun. A video of FBI history may be shown during the wait.

The Holography Collection
Address: 2018 R Street, NW (zip 20009) (map page 14)
Phone: (202) 667-6322
Hours: daily except Monday 11 to 6 except federal holidays
Admission: age 10 and up $9.50, under 10 $8.00, families $8.50 per person
Handicapped access: no—several steps down from the street to the entrance
Parking: metered street parking, some free but timed street parking nearby. Spaces usually limited.
Time needed: 1/2 hour

Location: south side of R Street between Connecticut Avenue and 21st Street. Metro (Red Line) to Dupont Circle (use Q St. exit), walk north 1 block on Connecticut to R, left 1/2 block.

This museum, established in 1983 and located in the basement of a row house, is owned by the Art, Science and Technology Institute. An air of secrecy pervades the entire guided tour: for security reasons, no cameras or note-taking is permitted, and you must ring the doorbell to enter.

The 20-minute guided tour is interesting enough, especially the three-dimensional light images created by lasers, mirrors, and photonic plates. You'll see samples of various holograms, such as a Ferrari with an opening door, a ballerina in motion (250 movements in a single image), and an insect under a microscope. The development and technology of holography are explained, however briefly.

While an informative presentation, one must question the unusually high admission prices in terms of what is offered.

National Building Museum

Address: 401 F Street, NW (zip 20001) (map page 14)
Phone: (202) 272-2448
Hours: Monday-Saturday 10 to 4, Sunday noon to 4; closed New Year's, Thanksgiving, Christmas
Admission: free; donations requested
Handicapped access: fully accessible
Parking: metered street parking
Time needed: about 1 hour
Location: north side of F Street between 4th and 5th Streets. Metro (Red Line) to Judiciary Square, walk north about 1 block on 4th or 5th to F.

The museum is housed in the beautiful Renaissance Revival style Pension Building, built in the 1880s to house the federal bureau that distributed pensions to disabled war veterans and the survivors of those killed in action. The building itself is worth a visit, even without the museum. A permanent exhibit describes its construction and history. The most impressive feature is the football field-sized Great Hall, which has been used for inaugural balls since 1885. The second and third floor balconies, which formerly held offices and now contain several of the exhibits, overlook the Great Hall. Guided tours of the building are given weekdays at 12:30, and weekends at 12:30 and 1:30.

This museum, established in 1980 by the U.S. Congress, commemorates the contributions to American life of the building trades. All aspects of the construction industry are explored: engineering, design, urban planning, historic preservation, and building materials.

Its mission is to show how the building process fits into the fabric of American life. It does so through changing exhibits and one permanent display, "Washington, Symbol and City". The latter is a hands-on interactive exhibit that shows the development of the "official" Washington, with its magnificent public buildings and open spaces that most visitors come to see, and that of the locals' city with its "working parts" and its social and economic challenges. The museum is also a repository of artifacts of the "built" environment—drawings and architectural photographs. There is a gift shop where you can buy postcards of the Pension Building, books on architecture and design, and other souvenirs.

National Museum of American Jewish Military History

Address: 1811 R Street, NW (zip 20009) (map page 14)
Phone: (202) 265-6280
Hours: Monday-Friday 9 to 5, Sunday 1 to 5 except Jewish and some federal holidays. Open Memorial and Veterans Days
Admission: free; donations requested
Handicapped access: fully accessible
Parking: metered and unmetered but timed street parking; spaces usually limited
Time needed: 45 minutes to 1 hour
Location: north side of R Street between 18th and 19th Streets. Metro (Red Line) to Dupont Circle (use Q St. exit), walk north 1 block on 19th, right 1/2 block on R.

This museum, under the auspices of the Jewish War Veterans of the USA, presents fascinating historical exhibitions documenting the courage, heroism, and sacrifices made by Jewish men and women who have served and continue to serve in the Armed Forces.

As a military history museum, its exhibits concentrate primarily on war-time subjects. Examples of recent offerings are "GIs Remember: Liberating the Concentration Camps", "Candid Moments in the Military 1914-1991", and "Major General Julius Klein: His Life and Work". The GI exhibit includes recorded reminiscences as well as photographs and other memorabilia of Jewish soldiers who were among the first to rescue survivors of the Nazi death camps as World War II ended. Because these are first-person accounts of men who had a religious bond with those they saved, this exhibit has a special poignancy, even to those who did not live through those times.

Upcoming exhibits will include "I Remember: Personal Recollections on the End of World War II, opening in May, 1995; "Philip Pearlstein: The War Years", opening in September, 1995; "JWV Celebrates One Hundred Years: 1896-1996", beginning March 15, 1996; "Women in the Military: The Jewish Perspective", opening February, 1997; and "Monticello, Jefferson, and the Jews: Commodore Levy's Impact on Social and Cultural Reform in America", which opens in February, 1998. The Museum invites contributions of letters, diaries, photos, and artifacts from the Revolution to the present to aid in its ongoing research documenting Jewish contributions to America's peace and freedom.

Without denigrating the contributions of other religious groups to America's military endeavors, the Jewish Military History museum relates a history that might otherwise go untold.

National Postal Museum

Address: 2 Massachusetts Avenue, NE (mail to: Smithsonian Institution, Washington, DC 20560) (map page 14)
Phone: (202) 357-2700
Hours: daily 10 to 5:30 except Christmas
Admission: free
Handicapped access: fully accessible
Parking: metered street parking, spaces usually limited
Time needed: about 1 hour
Location: north side of Massachusetts Avenue between North Capitol and 1st Street, NE, immediately west of Union Station. Metro (Red Line) to Union Station, adjacent to museum.

This is the newest of the Smithsonian's 15 Washington museums, opened July 30, 1993. It's housed in the lower level of the landmark City Post Office Building, a few blocks from the Capitol.

Here you'll see the largest collection of postal "artifacts" in the world, ranging from stamps to conveyances used to transport mail from colonial times to the present. There are six galleries, five of which are used to depict the history of the Postal Service. You start with "Binding the Nation", detailing mail service from pre-Revolutionary times through the Civil War. "Customers and Communities" covers the late 19th and early 20th centuries. Then move on to "Moving the Mail", where you'll see two airmail planes hanging from the ceiling and where you can walk through a railway mail car. Also on display are several delivery trucks in the evolution of motorized service. "The Art of Cards and Letters" puts a human touch on mail as a tool of communication, and "Stamps and Stories" features some of the museum's rare stamps and covers. Throughout the museum there are videos and photographic displays that help tell the Postal Service story.

Through interactive video, you can address postcards and greeting cards, and there is a museum shop for souvenirs as well as a stamp outlet. The museum also contains Discovery and Research Centers.

Textile Museum

Address: 2320 S Street, NW (zip 20008) (map page 14)
Phone: (202) 667-0441
Hours: Monday-Saturday 10 to 5, Sunday 1 to 5 except federal holidays and December 24
Admission: free; $5.00 donation suggested
Handicapped access: wheelchairs can be accommodated, but call first
Parking: free but timed street parking, spaces usually limited
Time needed: 45 minutes to 1 hour
Location: south side of S Street between 23rd Street and Massachusetts Ave. Metro (Red Line) to Dupont Circle, walk north on Connecticut Avenue about 3 blocks to S, left about 2 blocks on S.

The Textile Museum is housed in two adjoining Georgian townhouses just off Embassy Row. It was established in 1925 and now boasts more than 14,000 textiles and 1,500 carpets from around the world, dating from 3000 B.C. to the present. The collection was started by museum founder George Hewitt Myers, who also owned the two townhouses and lived in one.

There is literally always something different on display because many of the pieces are fragile and can be damaged by prolonged exposure to light and air. Therefore, exhibits are changed frequently. Recent offerings have included "Rugs and Textiles of Late Imperial China", "A Stitch Through Time: The Journey of an Islamic Embroidery Technique to Europe and the New World", and "From Kuba to Kars: Flat-woven Textiles from the Caucasus". If you're completely unfamiliar with the subject matter of a current exhibit, extensively detailed printed guides are available that not only explain the pieces but also give a brief background about the origin of the *genre* and define the nomenclature used in connection with it.

You may view the galleries on your own, but there are guided introductory tours on Wednesday, Saturday, and Sunday at 2PM from September through May Since the museum features little-known crafts and crafts-people, you'll probably gain much more from your visit if you take a guided tour.

An out-of-the-ordinary museum shop sells, in addition to the expected but tasteful note cards, tote bags and T-shirts, an unusual array of jewelry, clothing accessories, and an extensive selection of books on all aspects of rugs, textiles, related art, and how-to's on weaving, dyeing, silk painting, embroidery, knitting, and other crafts.

There is a garden behind the museum used for official functions, and a 15,000-volume library on the third floor; the library's hours are Wednesday to Saturday 10 to 2.

U.S. Department of the Interior Museum

Address: 1849 C Street, NW (zip 20240) (map page 14)
Phone: (202) 208-4743
Hours: Monday-Friday 8 to 5 except federal holidays
Admission: free
Handicapped access: fully accessible—wheelchairs enter on E St.
Parking: metered street parking, spaces usually limited
Time needed: about 1 hour
Location: north side of C Street between 18th and 19th. Metro (Blue and Orange Lines) to Farragut West (18th & I Sts.), walk south 6 blocks on 18th to C, right 1/2 block on C.

The present-day Interior Department was established in 1849 (is it purely co-incidental that that's also its street number?) and is now the umbrella agency for ten bureaus, all of whose stories are told in the museum.

The museum opened in 1938 and underwent a major renovation in the early 1990s. For security reasons, all adult visitors must show a photo-ID upon entering. The exhibits of the ten agencies extend the length of the long central corridor that forms the museum's core.

You'll see the work of each agency portrayed in over 1,000 specimens, 500 photographs, 100 models, 12 wall maps, 11 dioramas, 8 murals, and 1,450 labels. As you enter the main museum corridor you'll see a time line tracing the Department's history from 1775 to the present. After your visit, you'll understand why Interior has been called the Department of Everything Else.

This is an informative and well-crafted museum that explains just what Interior is and does.

U.S. Holocaust Memorial Museum

Address: 100 Raoul Wallenberg Place, SW (formerly 15th Street) (zip 20024) (map page 14)
Phone: (202) 488-0400
Hours: daily 10 to 5:30
Admission: free, but tickets required for most of museum (see details below)
Handicapped access: fully accessible
Parking: metered street parking, some free but timed parking on The Mall. Spaces usually limited.
Time needed: 2 to 3 hours
Location: enter on the west side of 14th Street between Independence Avenue and C Street, immediately north of Bureau of Engraving and Printing. Metro (Blue and Orange Lines) to Smithsonian (12th & Independence Ave.), walk west on Independence to 14th, left about 1/2 block.

This museum that tells the painful story of the Nazi Holocaust opened to much fanfare in 1993. Although there is no admission charge, tickets are required to view the permanent exhibits, and are available at the 14th St. entrance box office beginning at 10AM on a first-come, first-served basis. There is a limit of 4 tickets per person. Advance tickets may be obtained for a service charge from Ticketmaster, at (800) 551-SEAT (7328), (410) 481-SEAT (Maryland), (202) 432-SEAT (D.C.), or (703) 573-SEAT (Virginia). No tickets are required for the temporary exhibits, the Hall of Remembrance or Wexner Learning Center on the second floor, or the Resource Center or Wall of Remembrance, both on the concourse level.

The permanent exhibits are designed for persons at least 11 years old; younger children most likely would not understand the message of the Holocaust, and might be shocked by the graphic depictions. Even adults might find this and other parts of the museum terribly unnerving, particularly those who themselves or through close family members had direct experience with the Holocaust.

If you have children with you, begin with "Daniel's Story" on the first floor. This interactive video shows the transition from normal family life in German to ghetto to concentration camp as seen through the eyes of a young boy. The Wall of Remembrance is an exhibit of tile expressions produced by children. This, and "Daniel's Story", will probably produce in your children a basic understanding of the origins and meaning of the Holocaust.

A trip through the permanent exhibits begins with an elevator ride to the fourth floor. These exhibits, on this and the next two lower floors, recreate the Holocaust, beginning in 1933. The fourth floor theme is "Nazi Assault—1933 to 1939"). Two videos shown on this floor, "The Nazi Rise to Power" and "Anti-Semitism", put into words some of the photographs in the displays; both run about 15 minutes.

The third floor ("Final Solution—1940 to 1944") is undoubtedly the most moving part of the museum. It's built to look like a concentration camp. There are barracks from Auschwitz and Birkenau, a railroad car used to transport Jews to the camps, and a door to a gas chamber. Voices of Auschwitz survivors are continuously heard in the background. Not for the faint of heart.

The "Aftermath—1945 to Present" is the theme of the second floor exhibits. Here you will find listed the names of non-Jews who helped save Jews in Europe, the flags of armies that liberated the camps, and the Wexner Learning Center, which has 24 interactive computer stations that tell the Holocaust story in text, oral accounts, photographs, film, maps, and music.

The large two-level museum shop sells books, videos, posters, and other remembrances of the Holocaust. There is also a café in the administrative center on the 15th Street side of the museum. A first-floor donors' lounge has an interactive terminal where the names of persons who contributed funds to build the museum can be viewed.

The Holocaust Memorial Museum could fairly be described as a dramatic, yet reasonable and effective portrayal of an event unparalleled in world history.

Washington Dolls' House and Toy Museum

Address: 5236 44th Street, NW (zip 20015)
Phone: (202) 244-0024
Hours: Tuesday-Saturday 10 to 5, Sunday noon to 5
Admission: adults $3.00, seniors $2.00, 13 and under $1.00
Handicapped access: first floor accessible; second floor not accessible due to steps
Parking: metered and free but timed street parking
Time needed: about 1 hour

Location: near DC-MD line, on west side of 44th Street between Harrison and Jenifer, 1 block west of Wisconsin Avenue. Metro (Red Line) to Friendship Heights (Wisconsin & Western Aves.), walk 1 block west on Western to 44th, left 1-1/2 blocks.

This museum could be described as the contents of a collector's attic, but with an important difference: the collector in this case is a world-renowned authority on the subject, and the contents are authentic antiques, not reproductions. All items are identified as to subject, date, and origin.

Mrs. Flora Gill Jacobs, the museum's creator and director, has written several books on the subject of dolls' houses, which she started collecting in 1945. The museum opened in 1975 and comprises about half her personal collection of antique dolls' houses, toys, and games.

Most items in the museum are from the Victorian period. The houses are furnished in great but authentic detail. In addition to the houses, there are shops, schoolrooms, a "Zoo in Miniature" exhibit that had been loaned to Washington's famous zoo, an 18th-century German kitchen, dolls, and a substantial number of board games. The museum has the appearance of being cluttered because of the narrow hallways and walking spaces in this house-cum-office building, but the displays are all carefully organized with just enough space that they don't overlap each other.

There is a "birthday room" on the second floor, furnished as an Edwardian ice cream parlor, where children's parties are held. There is also a gift shop upstairs featuring dolls' house furnishings for beginners and collectors, books on related subjects, and consignments of antique dolls and toys.

As Mrs. Jacobs has said, the Dolls' House and Toy Museum is "dedicated to the proposition that dolls' houses of the past comprise a study of architecture and the decorative arts in miniature, and that toys of the past reflect social history." Her statement is a concise description of this museum.

MARYLAND

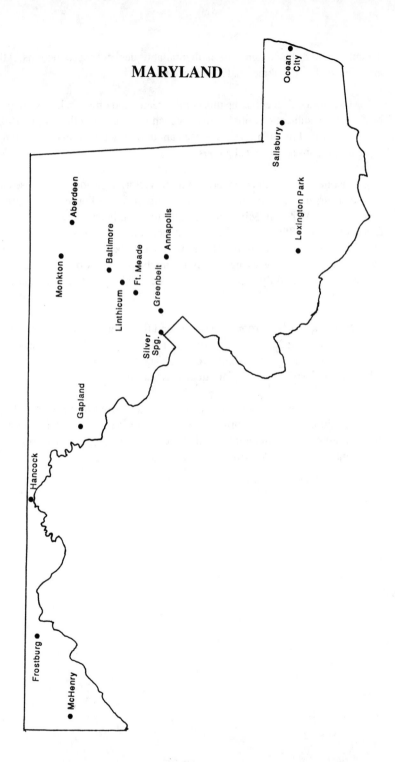

Ocean City

Salisbury

Lexington Park

Aberdeen

Baltimore

Monkton

Ft. Meade

Linthicum

Annapolis

Greenbelt

Silver Spg.

Gapland

Hancock

Frostburg

McHenry

Aberdeen (Harford County)

U.S. Army Ordnance Museum
Address: Aberdeen Proving Ground (zip 21005)
Phone: (410) 278-3602
Hours: daily 10 to 4:45, closed federal holidays except Armed Forces Day (3rd Saturday in May), Memorial Day, Independence Day, and Veterans Day
Admission: free; donations encouraged
Handicapped access: fully accessible indoors, wheelchairs may have difficulty reaching outdoor exhibits due to grass surface
Parking: free parking lot on premises
Time needed: 1 to 1-1/2 hours
Location: SE corner of Maryland and Aberdeen Boulevards. From I-95, take exit 85, follow SR 22 east for 3.7 miles to traffic light at Maryland Blvd., turn right for 0.4 miles to museum's parking lot on right. From US 40, take MD 22 exit, go east for 1.8 miles to traffic light at Maryland Blvd., turn right for 0.4 miles to museum's parking lot on right.

This museum highlights the Army's Ordnance Corps, which dates from 1775. It originated in 1918 in post-World War I France. The Calibre Board, charged with learning from the War's experience in the use of artillery, collected all kinds of equipment for evaluation. That equipment, and subsequent materiel, were shipped to Aberdeen for analysis, and the collection grew over time. In 1967, a group of local citizens formed a foundation to build a permanent home in order to prevent the by now large accumulation from being sold by the Army as a way of avoiding the cost of maintenance. The museum reopened at its present site in 1973.

The term "ordnance" includes the full range of weapons and ammunition used in warfare, and that's just what's displayed here. There are more than 8,000 artifacts that includes 260 large pieces, such as tanks. Nearly all the pieces are of World War I or later vintage. All items on display are identified as to name, model number, manufacturer, technical specifications, date of construction, and time and place of use.

The main floor houses rifles, pistols, mortars, submachine guns, aircraft machine guns, assault rifles, semi-automatic rifles, a few tanks, and Gen. Pershing's field car, a 1917 Locomobile. As you walk in you'll see a historical display case depicting the history of the Ordnance Corps from its 1775 beginning.

The balcony holds a display on the history of development of ammunition and of the machine gun as well as ammunition packaging and recoil rifles.

27

There are also small arms ammunition, howitzer casings, grenades, mines, World War II German signal pistol cartridges, shrapnel ammunition, and armor-defeating ammunition.

Be sure to walk through the 25-acre outdoor "Mile of Tanks" where some 225 tanks and trucks are parked. The weather has taken its toll on some pieces, and the museum foundation is trying to raise money to build a 300,000-square-foot indoor display area and classroom/theater.

There is a gift shop inside the museum selling books, mugs, scale models, and other souvenirs.

Annapolis (Anne Arundel County)

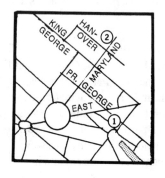

1   Tobacco Prise House
2   U.S. Naval Academy Museum

Tobacco Prise House
Address: 4 Pinkney Street (mail to: Historic Annapolis Foundation, 18 Pinkney St., zip 21401)
Phone: (410) 267-8149
Hours: see below
Admission: see below
Handicapped access: not accessible due to steps up from street
Parking: metered and free but timed street parking, and public lots in the area
Time needed: 15 minutes
Location: east side of Pinkney Street just north of City Dock

Tobacco Prise House is an unusual structure—a rare surviving example of an 18th century warehouse used to store tobacco harvested from the farms of

28

southern Maryland before it was sold and shipped to European markets. (Tobacco is still the chief cash crop in the area south of Annapolis.)

This warehouse has one ground-floor room measuring about 12 by 15 feet and a similar sized room upstairs, into which bales of tobacco were hoisted from the street using a long thick (about the size of a 4x4) wooden peg that protruded from the front of the building and served as a fulcrum.

Historic Annapolis Foundation is awaiting funding to reconstruct the exhibit inside, so consequently there is currently nothing to see other than the structural aspects of the building. Call HAF to find out if a date for reopening has been set.

U.S. Naval Academy Museum

Address: 118 Maryland Avenue (zip 21402)
Phone: (410) 267-2108
Hours: Monday-Saturday 9 to 5, Sunday 11 to 5 except New Year's, Thanksgiving, Christmas
Admission: free; donations accepted
Handicapped access: fully accessible
Parking: limited free parking in lot behind museum, free but timed street parking outside Academy grounds
Time needed: 1 to 1-1/2 hours
Location: Preble Hall at USNA, on north side of Maryland Avenue just inside Gate 3 (at Maryland and Hanover Street)

If it's important in American Naval history, it's here. The museum's founding dates from 1845 as the Naval School Lyceum, and has been in its present location since 1939. There are two large galleries on the main floor and an outstanding "Gallery of Ships" in the basement.

A chronology of the Navy occupies the main floor front gallery. The "time line" exhibits run clockwise around the room and include a variety of medals, letters, buckles, handguns, flags, ship models, and old documents (some from before 1800). John Paul Jones' linen tablecloth is here, as is the "Don't Give Up the Ship" battle flag from the War of 1812.

The rear gallery on the main floor displays portraits of admirals and lieutenant commanders, paintings of ships, a few ship models, uniforms and insignia, and ship gear.

Both galleries have personal memorabilia from famous and not-so-famous sailors, sculptures, photographs, swords, paintings, and prints interspersed with the other objects described above.

Most of the 108 models on display in the "Gallery of Ships", adjacent to the Naval Institute Bookstore, are from the collection of Col. Henry Huddleston Rogers and date from 1650 to 1850. Many are in their original display cabinets, and all are fully identified as to date, nation, and type. No two are exactly alike. Among the most unusual ships are models made from beef bones by French prisoners on English warships during the French-Anglo Wars (1756-1815). This part of the museum opened in 1993.

Baltimore (independent city)

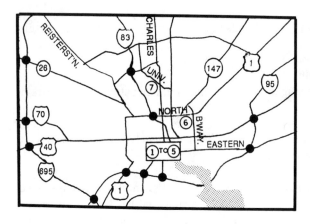

1 American Visionary Art Museum
2 Baltimore Public Works Museum
3 Center for Urban Archæology
4 Shot Tower
5 Dr. Samuel D. Harris National
   Museum of Dentistry
6 Great Blacks in Wax Museum
7 Lacrosse Hall of Fame Museum

American Visionary Art Museum (scheduled to open late Fall, 1995)
Address: 800 Key Highway (zip 21230)
Phone: (410) 653-5202 (until opening)
Hours (projected): daily 10 to 10 in summer, Wednesday-Sunday in winter
Admission (projected): adults $6.00, seniors and students $4.00
Handicapped access: fully accessible
Parking: metered street parking and public lot nearby
Time needed: about 2 hours
Location: SE corner of Key Highway and Covington Street, opposite Inner Harbor

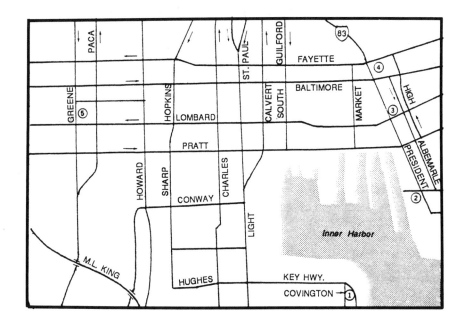

Visionary art is art produced by self-taught persons, often with no formal artistic training. It is, thus, the essence of the artist's feelings or visions rather than a deliberate attempt to create a particular image. Visionary artists are to this medium what self-taught inventors were to industrial progress a century ago. Their work has been called "outsider" art. That, in effect, is what will make this museum different from conventional art museums, and why it's been selected for inclusion in this book even before its opening.

This 36,000-square-foot museum will incorporate mostly new space into existing renovated industrial structures on the south side of Baltimore's Inner Harbor. It represents yet another innovative urban use in the city's showpiece of revitalization, and as such joins the National Aquarium, Harborplace, World Trade Center, and Maryland Science Center. The museum building will follow the curvature of Key Highway and will be shaped like a human heart, with an interior circular ramp creating a three-story column of light. It has already achieved architectural acclaim.

The American Visionary Art Museum was designated by Congress in 1992 as "the proper national museum, repository, and education center" for original, self-taught art. Ground was broken on November 28, 1993.

There will be six exhibition galleries, a tall (42-foot) sculpture barn, outdoor wildflower sculpture garden, theater, gift shop, research library, and gourmet café co-developed with Ben & Jerry's Ice Cream, Inc. The café will train handicapped persons to work alongside non-handicapped.

For further information prior to opening, write to Rebecca Hoffberger, President and Founder of AVAM, at P.O. Box 287, Stevenson, MD 21153-0287, or call her at the number above.

Baltimore Public Works Museum
Address: 751 Eastern Avenue (zip 21202) (map page 31)
Phone: (410) 396-5565
Hours: daily 10 to 5 June-September, Wednesday-Sunday 10 to 4 October-May
Admission: $1.50
Handicapped access: limited accessibility due to steps to main entrance, but arrangements can be made through advance phone call
Parking: metered street parking on most streets near museum, several lots and garages within a 3-block radius. Street spaces often limited.
Time needed: 45 minutes to 1 hour
Location: SW corner of President Street and Eastern Avenue, on east side of Inner Harbor

This museum looks at the city from the inside out by examining the working parts that the public never sees but takes for granted. It opened in 1982 in the former main city pumping station and is the first museum in America dedicated to the history of public works. Much of the museum is geared to school-age children, who make up a large percentage of the visitors, but adults would also find it educational and entertaining.

Slides and videos explain the operation of the water supply, waste disposal, and road and bridge construction systems. Photographic exhibits depict the changes in the city's infrastructure brought about by technological improvements over the years.

Baltimore's firsts in several public works developments—gas street lighting (1816) and earthen dam reservoir (1875)—are highlighted, as are more recent major projects, such as the 1985 Fort McHenry Tunnel that carries I-95 under the Patapsco River, the most expensive single project on the Interstate system. It's the widest underwater tunnel in the world and is the only one that curves in two directions at the same time.

Most exhibits change periodically, but two that remain constant are the "Construction Site", a hands-on area for children, and the outdoor "Streetscape", which is a full-size re-creation of underground utilities and above-ground street "furniture". Many 18th and 19th century public works artifacts that have been unearthed in modernization projects and construction and measurement tools used during the city's early history are preserved here.

One cannot help but leave with a greater appreciation for the unseen infrastructure that makes urban life possible.

Center for Urban Archæology

Address: 800 East Lombard Street (zip 21202) (map page 31)
Phone: (410) 396-3523 (weekends 396-4545)
Hours: Tuesday-Saturday 9 to 5, Sunday noon to 5 (4 PM closing Nov.-Mar.)
Admission: $2.00, free Saturday 10 to 1 only
Handicapped access: not accessible due to steps into building
Parking: metered street parking and public lots nearby
Time needed: 1/2 hour
Location: NE corner of Lombard and President Streets (I-83 extension)

Learning about archæology, specifically the urban variety, is the theme of this museum, one of seven historic sites in the city that operate under the umbrella "Baltimore City Life Museums". This particular National Register Historic building had been the home of Charles Carroll, a signer of the Declaration of Independence.

The Center was established in 1983 and has since excavated over fifteen sites in the city. The museum focuses on the techniques of archæology rather than on the results of the dig. There are a dozen "windows" in this relatively small (about 600 square feet) museum; each deals with a facet of the excavation process.

Start with "What Is Archæology?", where the technical terms are explained. The second window is an actual size (5 by 5 feet) excavation unit dug into the floor with artifacts placed in it in a way they might be found in the "field". Other windows show archæological detectives who are answering questions about what's been found using knowledge gained from similar previous sites, and laboratory processing (cleaning, sorting, coding, and cataloging, followed by a detailed analysis).

33

Artifacts from Baltimore's "Great Brewery Dig" of 1983 are on view in another window. Using an archæological trail guide from the museum, you can visit on foot several excavation sites within a few blocks; the largest of these is Brewers' Park, across Lombard Street from the museum, where the Peters/Clagett brewery produced beer for nearly 100 years, until 1879.

Great Blacks in Wax Museum

Address: 1601 East North Avenue (zip 21213) (map page 30)
Phone: (410) 563-3404, weekends 563-6416
Hours: Tuesday-Saturday 9 to 6, Sunday noon to 6, (5 PM closing Oct. 16-Jan. 14); open Monday in February, July, August, most federal holidays, and Martin Luther King Day
Admission: adults $5.50, seniors and college students $5.00, age 12-17 $3.50, age 2-11 $3.00
Handicapped access: first floor accessible
Parking: metered and free street parking
Time needed: about 1 hour
Location: on US 1 in north-central Baltimore, at SE corner of Bond Street, 2 blocks west of Broadway, 3 blocks east of Harford Road (SR 147)

This is the nation's first wax museum of African-American history, established in 1983 as a small traveling display and located since 1988 in a former city fire station. Its mission, according to founders Drs. Elmer and Joanne Martin, is to explain little-known but historically and culturally significant aspects of African-American history, to use great black leaders as role models for today's youth of all races, and to dispel myths of racial inferiority by focusing on the contributions of blacks to many areas of American life.

Appropriately enough, the entry lobby exhibits begin in ancient African and Europe. A walk-through slave ship tells the history of the Atlantic slave trade. The first two figures you'll see are Carter G. Woodson, historian who was the forefather of what has become Black History Month, and Bessie Coleman, the first black woman airplane pilot. This background sets the stage for the "walk toward dignity" in the rest of the museum.

The best place to begin is with the 8-minute video on the museum's theme and how it is presented. The video is shown in the basement theater. The exhibits, which follow a chronological sequence, are on the first and second floors. There are now some 120 figures ranging from Hannibal to Crispus Attucks, Harriet Tubman, Jackie Robinson, Malcolm X, and Shirley Chisholm, to many more lesser known persons such as Benjamin Banneker (inventor of the first clock built in the

U.S.), author Richard Wright, and modern-day civil rights leader Mary Church Terrell.

All figures are in appropriate period dress and in settings that demonstrate their contributions. Written documentation accompanies each display. But Joanne Martin stresses that visitors should look for the message presented by the displays, not just at the figures themselves. The museum takes a positive approach: it promotes blacks' contributions without detracting from those of other races or ethnic backgrounds.

The first floor displays highlight a wide variety of historical events and themes, among them the black church, Abolition, the Civil War, black reconstruction, western (U.S.) settlement, educators, the labor movement, military leaders, black nationalism, athletics, African statesmen, and the modern civil rights era.

The smaller second floor exhibit area highlights some outstanding Maryland natives and includes the museum's newest exhbit "And a Child Shall Lead Them", a special recognition of black youth as participants in the struggle for human rights.

Lacrosse Hall of Fame Museum
Address: 113 West Univerity Parkway (zip 21210) (map page 30)
Phone: (410) 235-6882
Hours: Monday-Friday 9 to 5 year-round, Saturday 10 to 3 March-May
Admission: adults $2.00, students $1.00
Handicapped access: fully accessible
Parking: metered and free street parking. Spaces often limited.
Time needed: 1/2 hour
Location: south side of University Parkway, between Charles Street and San Martin Drive/39th Street, adjacent to Johns Hopkins University

Lacrosse originated with North American Indians in the 1600s, and thus claims to be the country's first sport. Colleges began playing in 1877, when New York University fielded the first team. The National Lacrosse Association was founded two years later. The building stands on land donated by Johns Hopkins University and is also the home of the Lacrosse Foundation, chartered in 1959. Hopkins has long been a powerhouse in the sport.

The museum is organized on a chronological basis, beginning with the Native Americans. On display are rulebooks, vintage equipment, game programs, and photographs corresponding to points on the time line. Plaques commemorate milestones in the game' history. A trophy case lines one wall of the approximately 30- by 75-foot room, while another wall is set aside for changing exhibits. You can test your knowledge of the rules and history with the interactive lacrosse trivia game.

A 9-minute video "Lacrosse...The Spirit Lives" is shown in the auditorium just off the exhibit floor, and you can also watch replays from past games on the large screen.

National Museum of Ceramic Art and Glass
Currently closed pending relocation. Phone (410) 764-1042 for information.

The Dr. Samuel D. Harris National Museum of Dentistry (scheduled to open April, 1996)
Address: 31 South Greene Street (zip 21201) (map page 31)
Phone: (410) 706-0600
Hours: to be announced
Admission: adults $4.00, children $2.00 (projected)
Handicapped access: fully accessible
Parking: limited metered street parking, public lots and garages nearby
Time needed: undetermined
Location: at University of Maryland at Baltimore, on east side of Greene Street between Lombard and Redwood Streets

The Dr. Samuel D. Harris National Museum of Dentistry is named for a Detroit pediatric dentist who has long advocated preventive dentistry. To back up that commitment, Dr. Harris donated $1 million to help establish the museum. It's located at the home of the world's first dental school (1840) on UMAB's downtown campus.

The museum's mission is to educate the public about the history of the profession and the importance of preventive dentistry, and entertain people in the process. The museum will offer traditional exhibits as well as interactive displays.

George Washington's ivory dentures (not wood, as the legend goes) will be here, as will Queen Victoria's silver and mother-of-pearl dental instruments, a set of vulcanite dentures, and collections of dental keys (used to extract teeth). You'll also see the school's first diploma awarded in 1841 and a collection of toothpaste pot lids. Toothpaste originated as a powder and was stored in highly decorated pots, presumably to enhance its importance and value. There's also a varied collection of toothbrushes, ranging from sticks of wood to a wind-up mechanical model. Andy Warhol's four lithographs of Saint Appollonia, the patron saint of dentistry, will be on display. Exhibits also depict other tools of the trade such as tongue scrapers, fluoride, laughing gas, and local anesthetics.

A large part of the museum will be devoted to educating children on the importance of preventive care. Dr. Harris hopes that children may find the incentive to brush and floss after seeing the exhibits.

It seems as if this museum will be something you can really sink your teeth into. It promises to be different in orientation than the Historical Dental Museum in Philadelphia (page 123), so that the two will complement, rather than compete with, each other.

Shot Tower

Address: 801 East Fayette Street (zip 21202) (map page 31)
Phone: (410) 396-5894
Hours: see below
Admission: see below
Handicapped access: see below
Parking: metered and free but timed street parking, public lots nearby
Time needed: see below
Location: SE corner of Fayette and Front Streets, just east of I-83 extension

This National Historic Landmark is the last remaining of three shot towers in the city, built in 1828. It's scheduled to reopen in summer, 1995, following renovations; call for current status, hours, and admission charges.

Cannon balls were produced at this and the other towers by pouring molten lead through a sieve at the top into a tank of water at the base. Shot was produced here until 1892. The brick tower was built in less than six months without exterior scaffolding. It's 234 feet high, has a diameter of 40 feet at the base and 20 feet at the top.

Fort Meade (Anne Arundel County)

National Cryptologic Museum

Address: Colony 7 Road (zip 20755)
Phone: (301) 688-5849
Hours: Monday-Friday 9 to 3, Saturday 10 to 2, closed holidays
Admission: free
Handicapped access: fully accessible
Parking: free lot adjacent to museum
Time needed: about 1/2 hour

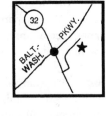

Location: at Fort George G. Meade, immediately east of Baltimore-Washington Parkway (SR 295). From the Parkway or I-95, take the SR 32 eastbound exit. Make the first left turn east of the Parkway, go 1/2 mile to museum on right.

One might say that this museum is devoted to secrecy. Actually, its theme is revealing secrets, particularly those used in military operations. The museum opened in 1993 and occupies its own building at the National Security Agency's headquarters, which fact may explain why no security clearance is required to visit.

The tour is self-guided—take a brochure when you enter and proceed to the numbered stops. Perhaps unintentionally, or perhaps to put you in a cryptological frame of mind, the exhibits were not arranged exactly as the brochure showed them when I visited, so you may have to do a little decoding of your own.

Cryptology as a modern science began between the two World Wars, but military intelligence using codes has been in use for several hundred years. You'll see a cipher wheel, believed to be the oldest such device in the world. Devices of this type were known in the 1600s, because Francis Bacon described one in 1605, as did Thomas Jefferson more than 150 years later.

Exhibits show the use of cryptology in World Wars I and II, including the machines used at the time. You can try your hand on a German Enigma. Other machines on display include the Sigaba, the only system used by any World War II participant to remain completely unbroken by an enemy; the Tunney and Sturgeon, the only known example of the Jade family of Japanese machines; and a Russian machine believed to have been captured from the Germans. The early use of computers in cryptology is explored in the Harvest exhibit.

Another exhibit shows the role of the "codetalkers" in World War II—American Indians who sent messages in their already encoded native language. Their system proved foolproof.

Although the brochure gives adequate explanations of the machines on view, the tour would be much more interesting if there were guides to conduct it.

Frostburg (Allegany County)

Thrasher Carriage Museum
Address: 19 Depot Street (zip 21532)
Phone: (301) 689-3380 or 777-5905
Hours: May-October: Tuesday-Sunday 11
to 4 (6 PM closing October only); April,
November-December: Saturday-Sunday
11 to 3; January-March and all other times
by appointment
Admission: adults $2.00, seniors $1.75,
children $1.00
Handicapped access: first floor only
Parking: lot on premises and across street.
Spaces may be limited.
Time needed: about 45 minutes

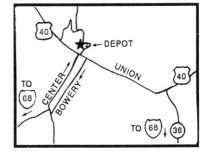

Location: opposite railroad station. Turn north down steep hill on Depot Street from Union Street (Alt. US 40) in center of town. Accessible by stairs from Union Street, where additional parking is available.

This relatively new (1992) museum is the culmination of work by local residents to display the extensive carriage collection of Jim Thrasher, a lifelong resident who died in 1986. His collection of more than 75 pieces was bought by Allegany County, and about two-thirds of it was placed in a restored 1800s warehouse.

A wide variety of horse-drawn wagons, carriages, carts, and phaetons are on view, most dating from 1890 to 1905. The oldest piece in the collection is a Germantown rockaway carriage from about 1850. In addition, there is a Park Trap carriage that Theodore Roosevelt once owned, as well as a five-glass landau used in his 1905 inauguration. You'll also see milk wagons, buckboard phaetons, delivery wagons, a hearse, one of the first golf carts, a firehose wagon, a tub cart, and mail wagons. No two pieces are exactly alike. There's a three-seated surrey (yes, with the fringe on top), and French, German, English, and Danish carriages. All the major carriage manufacturers of the late 19th century are represented, such as Brewster of New York City and A.E. Perren of Buffalo.

The carriages on display may be changed from time to time, since there isn't enough room in this building to house them all. The County is looking for additional sites to display the rest of the collection.

Gapland (Frederick and Washington Counties)

War Correspondents' Arch

Address: Gathland State Park (mail to Greenbrier State Park, 21843 National Pike, Boonsboro, MD 21713-9535)
Phone: (301) 791-4767
Hours: daylight
Admission: free
Handicapped access: difficult for wheelchairs because of grass surface
Parking: free lot opposite on Arnoldstown Road
Time needed: 1/2 hour
Location: Gapland Road at Crampton's Gap. Go east 1.0 mile from SR 67 or west 2.1 miles from SR 17 at Burkittsville to the top of South Mountain.

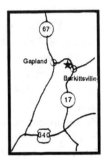

One would not expect to find such an imposing structure in this setting. The Arch was built in 1896 by Civil War correspondent George Alfred Townsend to honor his fellow correspondents. Their names are carved in concrete and embedded on the rear side. Townsend bought the land now occupied by Gathland State Park on which to build a retreat. The park was named for him—the letter "H" was added to his initials to form the Biblical place name Gath.

His original retreat, built in 1885, now houses a museum containing pictures of Townsend's original estate and books he had written. All but one of the other buildings built on the property are gone, except for the Arch.

The Arch is made of Hummelstown purple stone and is fifty feet high and forty feet across, with the pedestals about eight feet thick. The bottom Moorish arch is sixteen feet high, and the three Roman limestone arches above it are nine feet high and six feet wide at the base. These arches represent Description, Depiction, and Photography. A statue of the Greek mythological figure Pan with the traditional pipes stands in a recess at the height of the Roman arches. A square turret rises above Pan on the left side of the Arch to a top height of fifty feet. A smaller turret stands on the top of the right side of the Arch that formerly had a weathervane in the shape of a pen bending a sword. The weathervane is now in the museum.

Without question, a unique structure, and a well-kept secret.

Greenbelt (Prince Georges County)

Goddard Space Flight Center Visitors Center

Address: Soil Conservation Road (zip 20771)
Phone: (301) 286-8981
Hours: daily 10 to 4 except New Year's,
Thanksgiving, Christmas
Admission: free
Handicapped access: fully accessible
Parking: free lot adjacent to Visitors Center
Time needed: about 1 hour in addition to
1-hour tour

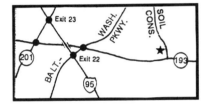

Location: Capital Beltway (I-95/495) exit
22 to Baltimore-Washington Parkway northbound. From Parkway (northbound or southbound) exit at Greenbelt Road (SR 193), go east 2.5 miles to Soil Conservation Road, turn left for 0.2 miles to entrance on left.

The main attractions at the Goddard Visitors Center are the hands-on spacecraft exhibits and the guided tours of the facilities. Be forewarned that only a few of the 37 buildings on the campus may be included on the tour; you may get to only one, either the Test and Evaluation Facility, Communications Network, Flight Dynamics Facility, or one of the satellite control centers. Guided tours are offered daily except Sunday at 11:30 and 2:30 starting at the information desk in the Visitors Center.

To acquaint yourself with NASA's work, take in the exhibits in the Visitors Center. These include "What Does NASA Do?", "How Do We Use Spacecraft?", and "How Do We Explore Space?" The kids will enjoy trying their hand at the manned maneuvering unit and the gyro-chair that creates the sensation of controlling spacecraft. All the exhibits use color photos, audios, and interactive video to explain the function of the various models on display.

In addition to the guided tours, the Center offers the following free regular monthly events:

•Model rocket launches—first and third Sundays (weather permitting), 1 PM. You may bring your own rocket.

•Discussions by NASA scientists or engineers on topics relating to astronomy, earth science, and space communications—fourth Sunday, 1 PM.

•Star watches—second Saturday, October through March, 7 to 9 PM, April 8 to 10 PM (weather permitting). Bring your own telescope or use theirs.

An extensively stocked gift shop is next door to the Visitors Center; the shop allows you to stock up on a wide range of space-related items, including models, books, games, and the usual run of souvenirs.

The Goddard Visitors Center is a great place for kids to learn about space exploration and the country's space program, but adults will also find it instructive.

Hancock (Washington County)

Sideling Hill Exhibit Center

Address: I-68, Hancock (zip 21750)
Phone: (301) 678-5442
Hours: Memorial Day-Labor Day: daily 8:30 to 6, otherwise daily 9 to 5
Admission: free
Handicapped access: fully accessible except for steps to ledge overlooking freeway
Parking: free lot on premises
Time needed: about 1/2 hour; add 15 minutes for walk to overlook
Location: at milepost 74 at top of Sideling Hill, 8 miles west of Hancock (not legally accessible by bicycle)

Many deep cuts in hillsides have been made in highway construction, but this is the only one where an exhibit center was built to "honor" the work that went into the building not only of this particular road, but of other similar engineering feats in general.

The four-level building opened in 1991 at the top of the first of several major mountains that highway travelers encounter heading west across Maryland. The 380-foot deep cut exposed 350 million years of rock strata, which make it an ideal geological "classroom". The oldest visible layers predate dinosaur fossils by 100 million years.

In addition to the expected photos and videos of the freeway's construction, there is a three-dimensional display of the cut, a wall mural describing and explaining the rock strata seen here, and a Maryland geologic map. There is even a display of roadkill—animals struck by cars. It's not nearly as gory as you might expect, but one has to question how dead creatures relate to the subject at hand. There are even rocks from the cut on sale.

If you're looking for exercise, you can climb the 100-or-so wooden steps on the north side of the highway for a closer view of the cut. Coin-operated viewers provide a panoramic view Appalachian ridge and valley zone to the north and east.

Lexington Park (St. Marys County)

Naval Air Test and Evaluation Museum

Address: SR 235 (mail to: P.O. Box 407, Patuxent River, MD 20670)
Phone: (301) 863-7418
Hours: July-September: Wednesday-Saturday 11 to 4, Sunday noon to 5; October-June: Friday-Sunday only, same hours
Admission: free; donations accepted
Handicapped access: fully accessible
Parking: free lot on premises
Time needed: about 1 hour
Location: north side of SR 235 opposite Shangri-La Drive, at Patuxent Naval Air Station Gate 2

This is the only museum in the country devoted to the testing and evaluation of naval aircraft. About a dozen planes (and one helicopter) stand guard on the grounds; all of them were tested here and all are identified by name and technical specifications. The museum was established on the Naval Air Station grounds in 1978 in a building originally built as a USO. Flight testing here began in 1943 after being transferred from the Anacostia Naval Air Station in Washington, DC.

Inside, you'll see conventional and unconventional testing and flying equipment. There are flight test instrumentation, a real-time telemetry processing system, the evolution of VHF/UHF radios in aircraft, and pilot's voice transducer. The latter measured the amount of force required to control a plane during test maneuvers. There are, of course, photos and models of early planes, including the Sea Dart Wind Tunnel model (1952), a Grumman XF9F-2 Panther Wind Tunnel Model (1947), Bell X-22A V/STOL research plane (tested 1970-1984), and McDonnell-Douglas A-3D. There are "cut-away" views of jet and turbo compound engines.

Among the unusual artifacts is a parafoil—it's packed like a parachute and opens to become a non-rigid wing capable of transporting the pilot long horizontal distances by virtue of its glider-like characteristics. There's also an XROE portable helicopter and a Goodyear Inflatoplane.

Jack Nial, executive director, says that as funds are available the museum will improve the signage explaining the role of display items in Navy testing. The museum is supported jointly by the Navy and the local community. Some funds come from the gift shop, where you can add to or begin your model plane collection or buy other souvenirs.

Linthicum (Anne Arundel County)

Historical Electronics Museum
Address: 1745 West Nursery Road (mail to: P.O. Box 746, Mail Stop 4015, Baltimore, MD 21203)
Phone: (410) 765-3803
Hours: Monday-Friday 9 to 3, first Saturday of month 10 to 2, closed holidays
Admission: free
Handicapped access: fully accessible
Parking: free spaces in front of building
Time needed: 30 to 45 minutes
Location: south side of Nursery Road, just east of Elkridge Landing Road, near BWI Airport. Take Nursery Road exit from Baltimore-Washington Parkway (SR 295), go west for 1.3 miles to museum on left.

The museum opened in 1983 and recently moved into its present quarters near Baltimore-Washington Airport. Exhibits are arranged by subject and cover the spectrum of sound reproduction and transmission from the days of cylinder phonographs to the space age.

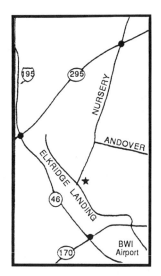

The tour is self-guided—pick up a gallery guide in the lobby. Because of the esoteric subject matter, much of the equipment may seem more like curiosities than readily recognizable items that you'd have everyday contact with. But all artifacts are identified and many exhibits are operable, facts which aid in understanding their function and use.

The development and uses of radar from its beginnings to recent alternatives are important parts of the exhibits. There's a large collection telling the history of airborne radar. You can climb inside the SCR-584, the first automatic tracking and gunfire control radar, which stands outside on the Nursery Road side of the building. The rotating SCR-270 radar that warned of the Japanese approach to Pearl Harbor in 1941 stands next to the SCR-584. A model of the lunar TV camera used on the first moonwalk in 1969 is here, too; it's one of only two in existence. You can try a German Enigma cipher machine (there's also one at the National Cryptologic Museum a few miles down the Parkway), or send a Morse code message to another gallery.

The museum has a spacious feel despite making efficient use of available space.

McHenry (Garrett County)

Cranesville Swamp Nature Preserve
Address: Cranesville and Lake Ford Roads (mail to: Nature Conservancy, 2 Wisconsin Circle, Chevy Chase, MD 20815)
Phone: (301) 656-8673
Hours: daylight
Admission: free
Handicapped access: may be difficult on boardwalk or trails

Parking: free lot on property
Time needed: 1 to 1-1/2 hours
Location: MD-WV border off
Cranesville Road, 10 miles west of
McHenry, 10 miles northwest of
Oakland, 12 miles south of I-68

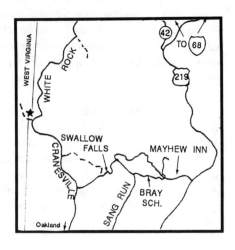

The Cranesville Swamp is
a feature highly unusual south of the
Mason-Dixon line. This National
Natural Landmark presents examples
of plant and animal life normally
found many hundreds of miles to the
north. The 560-acre preserve lies primarily in West Virginia, but the main
access and part of the property is in
Maryland.

The swamp (in reality a peat bog) lies in a basin on the Allegheny Plateau, 2560 feet above sea level. Because of the topography and a layer of hard
limestone that impedes drainage, the bog, like Canadian bogs, is perenially wet.
Cool air settling down at night from the surrounding hillsides causes the swamp to
be colder than the nearby higher elevations. This phenomenon supports plant and
animal life that could not survive in dry areas at this latitude, even on nearby
hilltops that are as much as 500 feet higher than the swamp.

The mountain earth snake and a northern water shrew are two of the rare
animals living in the swamp; the latter is said to be North America's smallest mam-
mal. The Nashville warbler, normally a denizen of Canadian bogs, is at the southernmost point in its breeding range here.

The red spruce forest in the swamp produces goldthread, a small ever-
green that grows as far north as Greenland. The bog fern, Canada yew, creeping
snowberry, and Jacob's ladder are other northern plant species that have been found
here. The swamp is home to the southernmost tamarack (larch) forest in the United
States.

Because of the wet and fragile nature of the preserve, visitors must stay
on the boardwalk and marked trails. There are four trails shown on the brochure
available from the dispensing box at the parking area. A 1,500-foot-long boardwalk leads into the heart of the swamp. The shortest route to the boardwalk is the

46

White Trail, a distance of about 1-3/4 miles round trip. Two other trails (Blue and Orange) circle the swamp, but both lead to the boardwalk.

Cranesville Swamp is without doubt one of the most unusual natural features of the mid-Atlantic region.

Monkton (Harford County)

Ladew Topiary Gardens

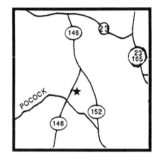

Address: 3535 Jarrettsville Pike (zip 21111)
Phone: (410) 557-9466 or -9570
Hours: mid-April-Oct. 31: Tuesday-Friday 10 to 4, Saturday-Sunday noon to 5
Admission: garden only: adults $6.00, seniors & students $5.00, children $1.00; garden and house: adults $8.00, seniors & students $7.00, children $2.00
Handicapped access: difficult in garden because of grass surfaces, house not accessible because of steps
Parking: free lot on premises
Time needed: 1 to 2 hours for garden, about 45 minutes for house
Location: east side of SR 146, 1 mile south of SR 152, 0.2 miles north of Pocock Road, 12-1/2 miles north of Baltimore Beltway (I-695) exit 27.

This country estate was the home of Harvey S. Ladew (1886-1976), a man born into wealth who spent most of his time doing things wealthy people do—collecting art, supporting charities, and keeping himself amused. In 1929 he bought a rundown farmhouse and accompanying acreage to have a place to stay while fox hunting in the Maryland hills. Over the years he converted it into a showplace, reflecting his refined but unusual tastes in art and decor.

The house tour (last tour one hour before closing) lets you transport yourself to Harvey Ladew's world—alas, temporarily. Throughout the place the art relates to fox hunting, as do the color schemes—mostly earth tones and dark greens found in forests. England is heavily represented, from the rare 17th century pine paneling for which the Elizabethan room had to be added, to the large collection of Staffordshire figurines and oval Chippendale partners' desk. Almost obliterated by the ubiquitous display of art, hunting memorabilia, and striking decor is the basic functionality of the house. Although it's a large place (Ladew added several rooms in order to create space for his acquisitions in England), every room had a distinct and obvious purpose. The highlight of the house is the oval library, which is in the book The 100 Most Beautiful Rooms in America.

He built the gardens to pursue his passion for topiary—the art of trimming shrubs and trees into ornamental shapes—developed on fox hunting trips in England. By the time of his death there were 15 distinct gardens covering 22 acres. The Garden Club of America has called this "the most outstanding topiary garden in America".

Follow the garden guide you'll get when you buy your ticket, and make your way to the Victorian garden, croquet court, rose garden, Garden of Eden (with statues of Adam and Eve), water lily garden, temple of Venus, Tivoli Tea House and garden (the façade of the tea house had been the ticket booth of London's Tivoli Theater), and sculpture garden, where you'll see Churchill's top hat and "V" for victory, sea horses, and a unicorn. In every season there is a different panorama of color.

You can make a day of your visit by having lunch in the café, taking in Ladew's painting and sculpturing studio, and visiting the carriage collection on the upper floor of the barn. The gift shop in the visitors' center sells a variety of plants, herbs, and other souvenirs.

Ocean City (Worcester County)

Ocean City Lifesaving Station Museum
Address: Boardwalk at the Inlet (mail to: P.O. Box 603, zip 21842)
Phone: (410) 289-4991
Hours: June-September: daily 11 to 10; May, October: daily 11 to 4; rest of year Saturday-Sunday noon to 4
Admission: adults $2.00, age 12 and under $1.00
Handicapped access: two steps to first floor, second floor not accessible
Parking: public lot adjacent to museum, meters operate during beach season. Spaces may be limited on busy days.
Time needed: about 1 hour
Location: south end of town along Boardwalk. Follow Coastal Highway/Philadelphia Avenue to its southern end, turn left for 1 block to museum on right.

The U.S. Lifesaving Service, a forerunner of the Coast Guard, once operated hundreds of stations along both coasts. This is one of the few remaining on the Atlantic coast, built in 1891, and is one of Ocean City's oldest buildings. Local men were hired to run the stations; their job was to rescue shipwreck survivors.

The local station is recreated in photos and memorabilia used by USLSS. There is a life car (a small rescue boat), log books, a nautical chart showing the location of shipwrecks off the Delmarva coast, and property salvaged from some of the wrecks. The inside of a surf boat, a larger vessel than a life car, can be viewed from a platform overlooking the main first floor exhibit room. Large murals depict how rescues took place.

Also on the first floor are a sand exhibit with samples from around the world and several aquariums with local marine life; you can feed the fish free every hour in the summer. Photos show the effects of two of the area's most devastating storms, in 1933 and 1962. A recent addition is the mermaid exhibit.

Upstairs displays consist primarily of locally significant mementos and events: china from old hotels, a bathing suit exhibit covering (or is "uncovering" a better term?) the period 1900 to 1960, a model of the Mayflower Hotel circa 1935 built as an open-back doll house, rolling chairs used on the Boardwalk, artifacts from the *Andrea Doria*, which sank off New England in 1956, and a seashell collection. A former highlight of Ocean City's Boardwalk was "Laughing Sal", a larger-than-life figure who stood in Jester's Fun House, a noted amusement.

When it's time to take a break from the beach, this is a good place to learn about the Ocean City that used to be. The museum has a gift shop selling lots of Ocean City souvenirs, jewelry, and nautical gifts.

Salisbury (Wicomico County)

The Ward Museum of Wildfowl Art
Address: 909 South Schumaker Drive (zip 21801)
Phone: (410) 742-4988
Hours: Monday-Saturday 10 to 5, Sunday noon to 5
Admission: adults $4.00, seniors & college students with ID $3.00, ages 5-18 $2.00
Handicapped access: fully accessible
Parking: free lot on premises
Time needed: about 1 hour

Location: southeast side of town, SE corner of Schumaker and Beaglin Park Drives. From center of town, follow signs from US Bus. 13 or US 50 to SR 12 (Snow Hill Road), go south for 1.4 miles, turn left on Beaglin Park for 0.5 miles to Schumaker.

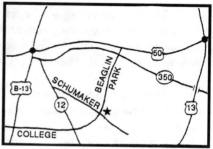

This is the world's largest museum devoted to wildfowl art, considered one of only four native American art forms. It opened in this dynamic building in 1992 after being housed at nearby Salisbury State University since its founding in 1975. The new location, appropriately, is on the banks of a pond where visitors can observe migratory birds feeding.

The museum highlights the work of the famous Ward brothers, Lem and Steve, who are credited with bringing the "working" decoy into the world of decorative art. Works of other carvers are also displayed, and there is an annual competition in April in Ocean City, 30 miles to the east. Waterfowl hunting has long been a mainstay of Eastern Shore life because its marshes and inlets attract birds on the Atlantic Flyway.

There are four galleries, three with permanent exhibits. These are "Decoy in Time", featuring a chronology of carving and hunting, including models of boats used by waterfowl hunters; "Wildfowl Championship Gallery", where award-winning decoys from the annual competition are displayed; and "Lem and Steve Ward Gallery" housing the brothers' work and a recreation of their shop. Unknown outside their native Crisfield, MD, until about 1948, the brothers were barbers who carved as a hobby before turning it into a full-time business.

You'll feel as if you're in the boat with the hunters as you walk through the marsh diorama. The museum also features two theaters where videos portraying the significance of carving as an art form and protecting wildlife habitats run continuously. There is also a workshop where carving seminars are offered for adults and children.

The museum has a consignment gallery and gift shop that features an attractive array of decoy-based mementos.

Silver Spring (Montgomery County)

National Oceanic and Atmospheric Administration

Address: 1325 East-West Highway (zip 20903)
Phone: (301) 713-2227
Hours: Monday-Saturday 8:30 to 5
Admission: free
Handicapped access: fully accessible
Parking: metered street parking, public lots, and
garages nearby
Time needed: about 15 minutes
Location: SE corner of East-West Highway (SR
410) and Colesville Road (SR 384), adjacent to
Silver Spring Metro station (Red Line). From Capi-
tal Beltway (I-495) eastbound, take exit 31, go
south on Georgia Avenue (SR 97) for 1.5 miles to
Colesville, right 3 blocks to East-West Hwy. From Beltway westbound, take exit
30, go south on Colesville Road (US 29) for 1.6 miles, cross Georgia Avenue (now
SR 384), go 3 blocks to East-West Hwy.

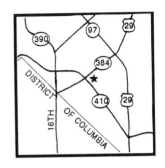

This is a small display protraying the work of the National Weather Service, a part of NOAA. It's located on the ground floor of an office building on the
west side of the Silver Spring Metro station.

You'll be able to check the weather forecast for all cities having NWS
offices on the video monitor. The current uses of satellite imagery and radar are
shown, and there are models of the TIROS satellite, which circles the earth fourteen times a day, and TOTO (totatile tornado observatory), which measures baro-
metric pressure, temperature, humidity, and wind speed and direction from the
ground—certainly better than sending a human out into a tornado to take those
readings. To show how far the Weather Service has come, there's a model of an
1891 NWS office in Cairo, Illinois.

You'll probably learn more about the Weather Service by visiting your
local office and talking to live meteorologists, but if there's no office near your
home and you happen to be visiting the Washington area, this is the next best
thing. A good place to visit if you have time to kill, but not something you should
go too far out of your way to see.

NEW JERSEY

Franklin

Ogdensburg

Haledon

Teterboro

Lyndhurst

W. Orange

Far Hills

Jersey City

Somerville

Highlands

Fort Monmouth

Trenton

Camden

Tuckerton

Egg Harbor City

Millville

Margate City

Ocean City

Camden (Camden County)

Campbell Museum

Address: Campbell Place (zip 08101)
Phone: (609) 342-6440
Hours: Monday-Friday 9 to 4:30
Admission: free
Handicapped access: not accessible due to steps at entrance, but call in advance to see if alternate access can be arranged
Parking: free parking lot in front of museum, but spaces often limited
Time needed: about 1/2 hour
Location: just east of downtown, about 1 mile east of Ben Franklin Bridge. Follow Campbell Place signs from I-676 or US 30.

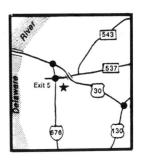

This museum, located at the headquarters of Campbell Soup Company, is devoted to soup tureens—all kinds of them. There are about 150 on display, dating from about 500 B.C. to the present. But the majority are 18th and 19th century European pieces, representing the peak period of decorative arts applied to tableware, and the height of formal dining among royal and aristocratic families.

Each piece is identified as to country, date, and construction. Most are earthenware, some are porcelain, and there are a few silver pieces. The dominant feature of the tureens is the variety of shapes. Many animals have served as models—turtles, ducks, water buffalo, rabbits, fish—as have vegetables and flowering plants.

Naturally, the contents of the tureens could not be enjoyed without a serving utensil, and these are just as exquisite as the bowls. Not all tureens are accompanied by ladles; but most of those that are on display, especially the silver ones, match the design of the bowl and were made at the same time.

The decor of the museum enhances the beauty of the collection. Each tureen is elegantly displayed on a glass (or plexiglas) shelf in its own "foyer"—a box with three black sides and a red "carpet" on the bottom.

With the exception of a changing exhibit, the displays are permanent. The changing exhibit features work by children in Campbell's outreach program in nearby schools.

Despite an obvious incentive to do so, Campbell deserves credit for not commercializing this outstanding and rare collection.

Egg Harbor City (Atlantic County)

Renault Glass Museum

Address: 72 North Bremen Avenue (zip 08215)
Phone: (609) 965-2111
Hours: Monday-Friday 9 to 5, Sunday noon to 5
Admission: free
Handicapped access: accessible, but with slight difficulty at doorways
Parking: free lot on premises
Time needed: about 1/2 hour
Location: NE of town. From intersection of US 30 and SR 50 in center of town, go east on 30 for 0.9 miles, left on Bremen Avenue for 2.2 miles to Renault Winery on right, after passing CR 561 and Alt. CR 561 intersections.

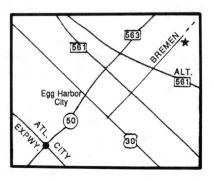

The attraction here is not the winery but the collection of wine and champagne glasses. Perhaps the priorities are reversed; there are plenty of wineries in the mid-Atlantic region, including several in New Jersey, but there's only one champagne glass museum. The museum is included in the winery tour, but it appears the collection is displayed primarily to give diners something to do while waiting for their table in the restaurant on the premises.

There are about 500 glasses on display, dating from the 16th century. Some surely must have belonged to royalty; if not, they should have, given their exquisite and finely detailed designs. Not all are identified, perhaps because the true origin is unknown.

Far Hills (Somerset County)

Golf House

Address: Liberty Corner Road (mail to: P.O. Box 708, zip 07931)
Phone: (908) 234-2300
Hours: Monday-Friday 9 to 5, Saturday-Sunday 10 to 4 except New Year's, Easter, Thanksgiving, Christmas
Admission: free
Handicapped access: fully accessible
Parking: free lot on premises
Time needed: about 1 to 1-1/2 hours
Location: south side of CR 512, 2.2 miles east of intersection of US 202. From I-287 exit 18, go north on US 202 about 2-1/2 miles to Far Hills, then right on CR 512. From I-78 exit 33, go north on CR 525 about 1 mile to Liberty Corner, then left on CR 512 for about 2 miles to entrance.

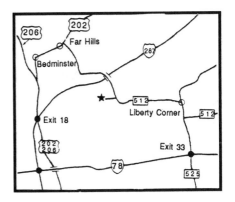

Although not named a Hall of Fame (that honor belongs to the one in Foxburg, Pennsylvania—see page 90), this museum surely is that, and more. The main building, a Georgian mansion designed as a residence by John Russell Pope (of Jefferson Memorial and National Archives fame), is home to the U.S. Golf Association, and, as you'd expect, houses an extensive collection of golf memorabilia. Many pieces were donated by the game's greatest legends—Gene Sarazen, Ben Hogan, Babe Zaharias, and Jack Nicklaus. There are old clubs, photos and portraits of U.S. Open winners, noted women golfers, turf maintenance tools, and interactive videos where you can test your knowledge of the game, find out about important events in USGA history, and play the 18th hole at Golf House.

Displays trace the evolution of golf equipment from its origins in Scotland in 1457, and include exhibits of ball making and club-making tools. The 6-iron used on the moon in 1971 by astronaut Alan Shepard is here as well. Two rooms are devoted to the life of Arnold Palmer (both as golfer and pilot), and another to Robert Tyre (Bobby) Jones. The main house also includes a 10,000-volume library—the largest collection on the subject in the world—and gift shop.

Even if golf and golf memorabilia don't particularly fascinate you, you're sure to find the Research and Test Center enjoyable. It's in a separate building about 100 yards from the main house. Here you can view how balls are produced and tested, and how the investment casting process is used in making clubs. Large windows let you see technicians going about their work. Interactive videos let you perform some of the same tests yourself. Among those you can watch are an initial velocity test and the aerodynamics lab with its wind tunnel and indoor test range.

Fort Monmouth (Eatontown) (Monmouth County)

U.S. Army Communications—Electronics Museum
Address: Kaplan Hall (Bldg. 275) (zip 07703)
Phone: (908) 532-2440
Hours: Monday-Friday noon to 4
Admission: free
Handicapped access: fully accessible
Parking: free lot adjacent to building
Time needed: 30 to 45 minutes
Location: south side of Avenue of Memories, opposite Sanger Avenue, 1.3 miles inside west gate of Fort Monmouth (SR 35 entrance). Museum is 0.1 miles west of Oceanport Avenue entrance (east gate) to Fort.

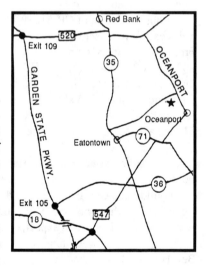

Since its founding in 1917, Fort Monmouth has been the headquarters for the Army's communications development. This museum tells the story of that development; tours are self-guided.

Equipment developed here is on display: World War I signal gear, the vacuum tube, combat photography equipment, radio equipped meteorological ballons, satellites, mortar-locating radar, and radio for military uses. Among these artifacts are the Lucky Strike spy cigarette camera and the Ohio Match box light meter, and the collection of vacuum tubes is quite rare.

Major Edward H. Armstrong, the pioneer of radio, merits his own exhibit. He discovered the AM and FM frequencies and his equipment on display is very rare.

Related products developed for the private sector as a result of initial research and testing here include solar batteries, walkie-talkies, and night vision devices.

The use of homing pigeons as a war communications tool is chronicled in a film in the museum's theater to the rear of the exhibit area; the birds were bred here for many years, but have since been superseded by more sophisticated equipment. The hero pigeon "GI Joe" is on display; he's known world-wide for saving over a thousand British troops under a bombing attack.

Tribute is paid to the Fort's commanders through photos and biographies in the Hall of Commanders; it also serves as a temporary exhibit gallery.

Franklin (Sussex County)

Franklin Mineral Museum

Address: 6 Evans Street (zip 07416)
Phone: (201) 827-3481
Hours: March-November: Monday-Saturday 10 to 4, Sunday 12:30 to 4:30; by appointment December-February
Admission: tour or collecting only: adults $4.00, seniors $3.00, school-age children $2.00; tour and collecting: adults $7.00, seniors $5.25, children $3.00

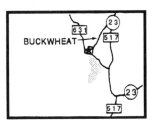

Handicapped access: fully accessible
Parking: free lot on premises
Time needed: about 1 hour
Location: about 1 mile west of SR 23—turn at traffic light onto CR 631, go 1.1 miles to Buckwheat Road, right 0.1 miles to Evans, left 0.1 miles to museum on left.

This museum is situated in the midst of the world's richest fluorescent mineral area, and its collection of same is the world's largest. An entire room is dedicated to these glowing rocks. In addition to native rocks, the museum features minerals from around the world, fossils, and Indian relics from the Americas.

The museum was founded in 1965 and expanded in 1990. It consists of two buildings: the newer one houses the displays and gift shop, while the older building is the zinc mine replica. (You will note that the former New Jersey Zinc

Company mine in nearby Ogdensburg is also described herein, but that mine was a different type of operation from this one.)

You have the opportunity to take home some of the rocks from the zinc mine; there is a collecting area behind the museum. The limit is 10 pounds per child and 25 per adult. If you don't find any that fit your fancy, fluorescent minerals (as well as jewelry made from them) are on sale in the gift shop.

Haledon (Passaic County)

Botto House/American Labor Museum

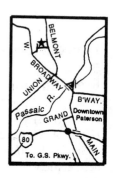

Address: 83 Norwood Street (zip 07508)
Phone: (201) 595-7953
Hours: Wednesday-Sunday 1 to 4 except major holidays, open Labor Day
Admission: age 13 and up $1.50
Handicapped access: first floor only, via rear entrance
Parking: free street parking
Time needed: about 1 hour
Location: 2 miles north of Paterson. From I-80 exit 57 to downtown Paterson, go north about 7 blocks on Main Street through downtown business district. Bear left at Broadway onto West Broadway, cross Passaic River, go 0.6 miles, bear right on Belmont Avenue for 0.8 miles, then left on Norwood for 2 short blocks. House is on NW corner of Norwood and Mason Avenue. From Garden State Parkway northbound take exit 155P, southbound take exit 159; both lead to I-80 west.

The history of the American labor movement, with emphasis on its development in Paterson, is commemorated here. One feature of the struggle in Paterson was that the immigrants of the early 20th century were skilled, economically middle-class workers and wanted to be paid appropriately. The factory owners needed their skills but did not want to raise wage rates above the level paid to the relatively unskilled employees they replaced.

This 1908 Victorian house is a National Historic Landmark, built and occupied by the Botto family. The Bottos were working class people from Biella, Italy, who immigrated to Paterson, which at that time was the center of the silk and dye industries in America. "Bunny" Kuiken, granddaughter of Pietro and Maria Botto, conducts the tours with first-hand perspective—she was born and lived most of her life in the house.

A 15-minute video sets the stage for your visit, giving a history of the labor movement in Paterson. The Botto House achieved its place in history as a result of the many labor rallies held here. During a 1913 strike, 20,000 silk workers stood in the street while union organizers addressed them from the second floor balcony. Upton Sinclair was one of the speakers.

The museum tries to mix the immigrants' lifestyle into the home. Some of the furnishings belonged to the Bottos. The period kitchen still has its original linoleum floor. Haledon, built on the slope of the First Watchung Mountain, was settled largely by Italians from the Piedmont region because it physically resembled their homeland. The Bottos had a grape arbor in the back yard, as they did in Italy.

The museum contains a library with writings on the labor movement. The second floor, which had originally been set up as two apartments, now houses changing exhibits.

Highlands (Monmouth County)

Twin Lights Historic Site
Address: Highlands Avenue (zip 07732)
Phone: (908) 872-1814
Hours: Wednesday-Sunday 10 to 5; grounds open 9 AM to
dusk year-round
Admission: free
Handicapped access: outside only
Parking: free lot on premises
Time needed: 30 to 45 minutes

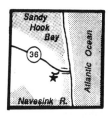

Location: just of SR 36, overlooking Sandy Hook Bay and Atlantic Ocean. From SR 36 southbound (eastbound), make sharp right turn immediately before Navesink River drawbridge onto Portland Avenue, immediately right again uphill on Highlands Avenue for 0.1 miles, bear left uphill on Light House Road for 0.2 miles to top of hill. From SR 36 northbound, cross drawbridge, then immediately sharp right down hill, right under bridge, and right uphill, cross Portland Avenue and continue uphill as above. From Garden State Parkway exit 117, take SR 36 east about 13 miles to Highlands.

Twin Lights is unique because of its structure. The brownstone towers and connecting building were of much more substantial construction that most other lighthouses on the coast, and the fact that there were two lights also made this site unique.

The present towers were built in 1862, but the first lighthouse was confirmed as early as 1828 and a second one in 1841. Twin Lights holds a number of "firsts" among lighthouses: first use (in 1841) of the revolutionary Fresnel lenses, first to be fueled (in 1883) by kerosene, and first use of electric power (1898).

Twin Lights had a strategic position protecting Lower New York Bay. At 200 feet above sea level, this is the highest elevation directly on the Atlantic coast south of New York. The panorama of the Bay, Sandy Hook, and New York City is alone worth the visit. If the view from the grounds isn't good enough, you can climb about 50 feet higher in the North Tower for a better look. The South Tower is open only when staff is available.

The museum contains exhibits of navigational instruments, a life car (the small rescue boat used by the U.S. Life Saving Service), and other mementos of the days when this was a USLSS station. The 1862 architect's drawings of the lights are also on display.

Outside, a plaque commemorates the first wireless telegraph in the U.S., for which Gugliemo Marconi built a mast here in 1899, and there is a boat exhibit in a separate building built in 1849 as the Spermaceti Life Saving Station and moved here from its original site at Sandy Hook.

Jersey City (Hudson County)

Statue of Liberty and Ellis Island Immigration Museum
Address: Liberty State Park (mail to: Liberty Island, New York, NY 10004)
Phone: (212) 363-3200; ferry (212) 269-5755
Hours: daily 9 to 5, later in summer
Admission: both free. Ferry (round trip): adults $7.00, age 3-17 $3.00
Handicapped access: both fully accessible except from pedestal to top of crown of Statue
Parking: $4 fee at ferry dock, refunded for stays under 2 hours
Time needed: at least 3 hours, plus ferry rides and waiting times at ferry and Statue
Location: From NJ Turnpike exit 14B, turn left after leaving toll booth, go 0.8 miles to Freedom Way, turn left for 0.9 miles to Audrey Zapp Drive, right to ferry dock on left, parking lot on right. Statue and Ellis Island accessible only by ferry from Liberty State Park or Battery Park in New York City.

The Statue of Liberty and Ellis Island, while normally associated with and territorially part of New York City, physically lie within New Jersey waters and are accessible from New Jersey, hence, they qualify for inclusion in this book on geographical terms. Moreover, each is unique in its own right—the Statue for obvious reasons, and Ellis Island for its Immigration Museum.

Neither the Statue or Ellis Island are places to go to if you have an hour or two to kill. Not only will you need to allow enough time to visit (and you might as well do both in one trip for the same ferry fare), there will be waiting lines on many days. If you hate to wait, you probably should pick a rainy day in winter.

The ferry stops first at the Statue. The ground floor holds the souvenir shop. An immigration exhibit on the second level shows an immigrant's perspective on his or her arrival in America. Another tells the Statue's story, from conception of the idea through construction, and restoration in time for her centennial in 1986. There is also a full-scale copper replica of one of Liberty's feet.

There are 354 steps from the top of the pedestal to the crown. The pedestal is 89 feet high, sufficient for a dramatic view of the Harbor and lower Manhattan. The Statue rises another 151 feet.

The ferry ride to from the Statue to Ellis Island takes about 10 minutes. Ellis was the place where 17 million immigrants first set foot on American soil. They were given physical and mental tests to determine their right to enter the country. If they failed, they were sent back to their native land on the next boat. The processing center operated from 1892 to 1954, and in 1990 was restored to the way it looked in the early 1920s.

The Immigration Museum has an obviously similar theme to the exhibits at the Statue, but shows in greater detail and from a broader perspective what it was like to arrive in America for the first time. A sampling of personal and household items the immigrants would have brought are displayed—ordinary clothing, native costumes, musical instruments, toys, and trade and household tools. Photos capture the emotions these people felt, and there are films and oral histories that tell their story in ways a mere photograph cannot. Outside on the promenade is the American Immigrant Wall of Honor inscribed with the names of 400,000 people who passed through the center. If you're among the 40 percent of Americans whose ancestors entered through Ellis Island, there's about a 2-1/2 percent chance that you'll find one or more of your relatives' names here.

Both the Statue and Immigration Museum epitomize the vision that America represented to the parents and several generations of grandparents of millions of us. It's good to look at our country from their perspective, and there's no better place to do that than here.

Lyndhurst (Bergen County)

Hackensack Meadowlands Environmental Center (Trash Museum)

Address: 2 DeKorte Park Plaza (zip 07071)
Phone: (201) 460-8300
Hours: Monday-Friday 9 to 5, Saturday 10 to 3
Admission: $2.00, children under 12 free
Handicapped access: fully accessible
Parking: free lot on premises
Time needed: 1/2 to 1 hour
Location: east of SR 17 just south of SR 3 interchange. Turn east off 17 at Polito Avenue traffic light, go 0.5 miles to Valleybrook Avenue, then left for 1.7 miles to entrance on right.

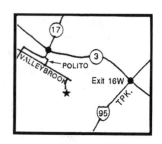

That's right, a museum devoted to trash, the first of its kind in the country. It's oriented mainly to kids, but there are lessons adults could also profit from. Built on a landfill that eons ago was the Hudson River, the Environmental Center protects an ecologically important zone in the midst of the New York metropolis. The Trash Museum, opened in 1989, exists to increase awareness of the problem of garbage disposal and its effect on the environment.

The exhibit themes are cleverly arranged and presented. They deal with "How Far Does Your Trash Travel?", "Recycled-But Good as New", and "Ideal Town". All the displays are hands-on, making them fun and educational for the kids, but not losing the message for adults. For example, as you pass an exhibit of various types of trash, a child's voice automatically comes on and a part of the display lights up to tell how much of each type of trash each person throws away every day. Another visual shows the amount of trash produced for various consumable products—one cookie, for example. Lighted boxes show where different wastes go.

In the main lobby there is a 30-by-7 foot diorama of an urban salt marsh, such as the one adjacent to the museum. The "live" creek holds snapping turtles, crabs, grass shrimp, and diamondback terrapins. Mounted, not live, specimens show the animal species inhabiting the Meadowlands. Photos are posted of birds that are likely to be sighted outside the museum during the current month; over 250 species have already been seen.

The Marsh Discovery trail, a boardwalk nearly completely circling the marsh begins at the edge of the parking lot. This trail connects with the Transco Trail, which completes the loop back to the museum. Transco is a 20-foot wide dike along the route of a natural gas pipeline.

The museum has a gift shop selling books, cards, scented soaps, seeds, and other recycled products.

Margate City (Atlantic County)

Lucy the Elephant

Address: 9200 Atlantic Avenue (mail to: P.O. Box 3000, zip 08402)
Phone: (609) 823-6473; 822-6519
Hours: April-mid-June, and September-October: Saturday-Sunday 10 to 4:30; mid-June through Labor Day: daily 10 to 8:30
Admission: adults $2.00, children $1.00
Handicapped access: ground level only
Parking: free lot on premises, metered street parking
Time needed: about 1/2 hour

Location: SE corner of Decatur and Atlantic Avenues, 1 block from beach, about 3 miles south of Atlantic City. From mainland, take CR 563 (toll bridge) onto Jerome Avenue in Margate City to right on Atlantic for about 4 blocks to Decatur.

This 65-foot high National Historic Landmark was built in 1881 and used as a hotel and tavern until the early 1900s. The howdah (the canopied seat atop the elephant) stood at the height of a six-story building as was used to provide an expansive view of the coastline. Lucy was a prime attraction until after World War II, and finally was closed in the early 1960s. A group of local citizens rescued Lucy after she was donated to the city of Margate, and restoration began in 1973. The exterior was completed four years later, but the interior spaces and howdah remain to be completed.

Restorations are suspended during the season when Lucy is open to visitors. Souvenir sales of commemorative books, Lucy shot glasses, key chains, pewter magnets and sculptures, pendants, T-shirts, and sweatshirts help finance reconstruction.

Millville (Cumberland County)

Museum of American Glass

Address: 1501 Glasstown Road (zip 08332)
Phone: (609) 825-6800
Hours: April-December: daily 10 to 5; January-March: Wednesday-Sunday 10 to 5. Closed New Year's, Easter, Thanksgiving, Christmas
Admission: adults $6.00, seniors $5.50, students $3.50, under 5 free, family $12.00; all categories $1.00 less (family rate $2.00 less) January-March. No charge to stroll the grounds or shop except on special events days.
Handicapped access: fully accessible
Parking: free lot on premises
Time needed: 1 to 1-1/2 hours
Location: NE part of town. From center of town, go east on Broad Street (CR 552 Spur) to Wade Blvd., turn left for 0.6 miles.

Carl Sandburg, in "Reckless Ecstacy" wrote: "Down in southern New Jersey they make glass. By day and by night, the fires burn on in Millville...." When you visit the Museum of American Glass, you might think every piece of glass ever made in Millville is on display here. The museum has 7,500 pieces on view, in chronological order starting with glassmaking in Jamestown, Virginia, in 1608, and continually virtually to today.

The museum is part of Wheaton Village, which could be described as the Sturbridge Village of New Jersey. In addition to the museum, there are about a dozen shops lining the main walk, selling books, pottery, candy, and, of course, glassware.

But the main attraction is the museum, housed in a colonnaded one-story building that has a distinct Southern architectural appearance. As you move through the glassmaking "time zones" you'll see distinct changes in the types of specimens exhibited. It's easy to follow along, because all pieces are identified and dated, with explanations of the history of the type.

64

There are cut glass, carnival (poor man's Tiffany) glass, paperweights, tableware, mason jars, glass kitchen utensils and containers, decorative art glass, marbles, wine and liquor bottles, lustre art, and more. One room is devoted to pressed glass from the 1825-1850 period, another to contemporary designs made at the Creative Glass Center of America established here in 1983. The world's largest bottle, measuring 7'8" tall and holding 188 gallons, was made here in 1992.

A well-rounded history of glassmaking in America is provided, with biographies of "gaffers" (they're journeyman artisans), photos of factories both nearby and elsewhere, and exhibits displaying commercial and industrial uses of glass.

Three times a day, at 11, 1:30, and 3:30, you can watch a 20-minute demonstration of glass blowing in the replica of an 1888 factory, located behind the museum. If you like what you see being made, you can buy a sample in one of the Village shops. You can even make an appointment to make your own paperweight, but call in advance. There are frequently special events at the Village, some having nothing to do with glass, but the expansive grounds provide an ideal venue for them, and of course, draw people to the shops and museum.

If you can visit only one glass museum, this should be it.

Ocean City (Cape May County)

Discovery Seashell Museum
Address: 2721 Asbury Avenue (zip 08226)
Phone: (609) 398-2316
Hours: mid-May—mid-October: Monday-Saturday
9 to 8, Sunday 9 to 6; closed rest of year
Admission: free
Handicapped access: fully accessible
Parking: free street parking. Spaces may be limited
in summer.

Time needed: 1/2 to 1 hour
Location: east side of Asbury Avenue between 27th and 28th Streets, about 3 blocks from beach. From Garden State Parkway exit 25, go east on CR 656, which is 34th Street in Ocean City, turn left on Asbury for 6-1/2 blocks.

This museum has the largest seashell collection in the world—that pretty much sums it up. In addition, there is a live marine tank, minerals, fossils, and corals. The museum is also a gift shop, but it's the display of the shells, not the sale of them, that dominates. A good diversion on rainy beach days.

Ogdensburg (Sussex County)

Sterling Hill Mining Museum

Address: 30 Plant Street (zip 07439)
Phone: (201) 209-7212
Hours: April-November: daily 10 to 5; March &
December: Saturday-Sunday 10 to 5 and by ap-
pointment, weather permitting; open Christmas
week 10 to 5. Mine tours 1 and 3 PM.
Admission: adults $7.50, seniors (age 65 & over)
$6.50, under 17 $5.00
Handicapped access: fully accessible, but with
some difficulty in mine
Parking: free lot on premises
Time needed: 2-1/2 hours including mine tour
Location: turn west off CR 517 in center of town onto Passaic Avenue, go 0.7
miles to entrance on left, just past intersection of Plant Street/Cork Hill Road

This museum has developed at the former New Jersey Zinc Company
mine, which was closed in 1986 due to poor economic conditions and a property
tax dispute with the borough of Ogdensburg. Actually, mining here is thought to
have been conducted by the Dutch in 1640, and possibly even earlier by local
Indians, although obviously not in the same way that modern mining was done.
Following the mine's abandonment by New Jersey Zinc, it was bought by brothers
Robert and Richard Hauck, who, with the help of concerned local citizens, restored the property so it could be opened to the public. The museum opened in
1990 and is a National Historic Site.

This is the only underground mine tour in New Jersey. While there are
some similarities to coal mining in Pennsylvania, the techniques used in this mine,
and the way the tunnels have been dug, are somewhat different, so you cannot say
that if you've seen one mine, you've seen them all.

The tour begins in the museum, located in what was called the "drying
house" because miners hung their wet work clothes there overnight to dry. This
particular building was built in 1937. Part of the building is just as it would have
appeared while the mine was active, with miners' lockers, the shower room, and

the hanging baskets into which they put their wet clothing. The rest of the space holds mining tools, lamps, drill bits, other mining memorabilia, and Thomas Edison's inventions that related to mining. A large collection of minerals is also exhibited (if you've been to the Franklin Mineral Museum, or read its description a few pages back, you know that this area contains the world's richest supply of fluorescent minerals—over 335 species have been identified, 35 of which exist nowhere else).

After you've been acquainted with the tools and artifacts of mining, it's time to go into the tunnel. The mine is a constant 45 degrees and damp, so a jacket will feel good. Unlike the coal mine tours of Pennsylvania, this one stays at approximately the same elevation as where you entered because the orebody was exposed by erosion, eliminating the need for deep vertical drilling. So instead of going down into the earth, you go farther into the hillside.

The mine tour guide, usually Richard Hauck, gives an informative description of mining methods used here. At one point everyone is invited to pick up a rock from the floor. The lights are then turned off and an ultraviolet lamp turned on so you can see your fluorescent rock glow. In 1995 a third tunnel, 640 feet long, will be added to the tour.

After your tour, you can visit the gift shop for more mineral specimens to add to your collection, or for other souvenirs.

Somerville (Somerset County)

U.S. Bicycling Hall of Fame
Address: 166 West Main Street (zip 08876)
Phone: (908) 722-3620; (800) BICYCLE (242-9253)
Hours: Monday-Friday 9 to 5 except holidays
Admission: free; donations accepted
Handicapped access: fully accessible
Parking: metered street parking and public lots nearby
Time needed: about 1/2 hour
Location: downtown, north side of Main Street (SR 28) between Doughty and Davenport Avenues

This museum, established in 1987, is still in its infancy. Plans are being considered to relocate to a larger facility on the south side of town. The museum is presently on the ground floor of a small but modern office building and lacks room to expand.

Somerville is the scene of the "Tour of Somerville", an annual Memorial Day race begun in 1940, hence the selection of the town for the museum. It's primarily racing oriented because non-competitive bicyclists rarely acquire the kinds of mementos for their endeavors that racers win, and which become the blocks on which museums are built. So what you'll see here are trophies, medals, photographs of six-day racers, racing magazines and programs, and track bikes.

These bikes were originally used on indoor velodromes, such as at Madison Square Garden in New York, where the famous six-day races were held. They differ from conventional bikes in that they have only one gear and no freewheel, meaning they can't coast and the pedals turn whenever the wheels move. They also lack brakes; to slow down or stop, the rider pushed hard against the rotation of. the pedals. The 1910-era track bikes on view here are strikingly similar to track bikes of today, and nearly as light in weight.

The Hall presently has 25 inductees, whose pictures line one wall. Most are or were racers, but several were elected for their off-the-bike contributions to the sport: Colonel Albert Pope, who pioneered bicycle manufacturing in America; and Robert Rodale, chairman of Rodale Press, publisher of "Bicycling" magazine and benefactor of the Lehigh County Velodrome in Trexlertown, Pennsylvania.

Despite limited space, the museum maintains a small area where bicycle-related mementos (T-shirts, caps, lapel pins, water bottles) are sold.

Teterboro (Bergen County)

New Jersey Aviation Hall of Fame
Address: Industrial Avenue (zip 07608)
Phone: (201) 288-6344
Hours: Tuesday-Sunday 10 to 4
Admission: adults $3.00, seniors and children under 12 $2.00
Handicapped access: east building fully accessible, west building not accessible due to steps to tower
Parking: free lot on premises at both locations, space may be limited at west building
Time needed: 1 to 1-1/2 hours

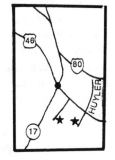

Location: at Teterboro Airport on south side of US 46, just east of SR 17. For east building, turn south off 46 at Huyler Street traffic light onto Fred Wehran Drive, go 0.4 miles to museum. For west building, turn south off 46 at Industrial Avenue traffic light, go 0.5 miles to entrance on left.

This museum has two sites, at least for the time being. The main exhibits are in the east building, located on the east side of Teterboro Airport. This building is being expanded, with the addition that will quadruple its size scheduled to open in July, 1995.

The second site is in the airport's old control tower on the west side of the field. It contains the old tower equipment (non-operational now, but you can still listen to controllers working from the new tower across the field) and pictorial exhibits honoring New Jerseyans important in aviation—Lindbergh, Earhart, Aldrin, Schirra, and others. But be prepared for about a 4-flight climb to the tower.

The Aeronautical Educational Center in the east building has better displays telling the history of aviation, particularly as it relates to or occurred in New Jersey. Models of every engine made by Curtiss-Wright, the X-15 used in moon flights, World War I and II equipment, a propeller from an NC-4, the first plane to fly the Atlantic (1919), a wheel from a moon Land Rover, and Walter Schirra's space suit are among the items on view. In addition, there are exhibits commemorating the contributions of women in aviation, transatlantic air mail service (originally out of Hadley Field in South Plainfield, now gone), the Flying Tigers, and the building of propellers here by Wright Aeronautical, predecessor of Curtiss-Wright.

You may touch many of the artifacts, and outside, you can walk aboard a Martin-202 plane. The expansion will permit the museum to display more of its aircraft collection indoors and to improve the arrangement of the existing exhibits.

Trenton (Mercer County)

State Police Museum and Learning Center

Address: River and Trooper Roads (mail to: P.O. Box 7068, W. Trenton 08628)
Phone: (609) 882-2000
Hours: Monday-Friday 10 to 4
Admission: free
Handicapped access: fully accessible

Parking: free lot adjacent to museum
Time needed: about 45 minutes
Location: just off I-95 and SR 29. From
I-95 exit 1, follow signs for SR 29 south,
which requires going north briefly, then
making U-turn onto River Road. Go south
on River Road for 0.5 miles, left on
Trooper Road for 0.2 miles to museum.

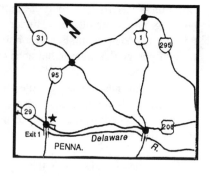

This museum is unusual in that
it depicts the history and operation of a
state police force. The museum began in
a log cabin built in 1934 as a Depression-era Civilian Works Administration project
that was, appropriately enough, a State Police dormitory and training center. But
by 1992 the exhibits had outgrown the cabin and a new building was built and
connected to the cabin by an enclosed walkway. The museum was founded in
1984 after the Lindbergh kidnapping files were opened; they needed a place to be
displayed, and since the State Police had investigated and solved the crime, the
files found a home here.

The New Jersey State Police was founded in 1921. Most exhibits focus
on its current activities rather than its history, although there are displays of uniforms worn and weapons used through the years, and the aforementioned effects
from the Lindbergh kidnapping in 1932 (the first Superintendent of the State Police, and still in office at that time, was Col. H. Norman Schwarzkopf, father of the
hero of the 1991 Persian Gulf war).

Other displays are of confiscated weapons, drug interdictions, Mafia wire-
taps, the science of fingerprinting, how the 9-1-1 emergency response system
works, missing persons, and an interactive display on finding evidence at crime
scenes.

In the log cabin are two police cruisers—a 1991 model and a 1930 Buick
that was restored and sold back to the State Police a few years ago, and 1921 and
1948 Harley-Davidson motorcycles. One room in the cabin is set up as a trooper's
bedroom; until 1976, troopers lived at the barracks to which they were assigned.
The rest of the space is now used as a classroom.

Tuckerton (Ocean County)

Barnegat Bay Decoy and Baymen's Museum

Address: Main Street (mail to P.O. Box 52, zip 08087)
Phone: (609) 296-8868
Hours: Wednesday-Sunday 10 to 4:30
Admission: age 12 and over $2.00
Handicapped access: fully accessible
Parking: free lot on premises
Time needed: 30 to 45 minutes
Location: west side of US 9 at entrance
to Stanley Tip Seaman County Park. From
Garden State Parkway northbound, take
exit 50 and follow US 9 north for 7 miles;
southbound take exit 58, left on CR 539
for 3 miles to US 9, right for 0.2 miles to
museum.

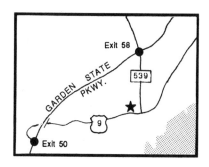

This new museum's (it opened in July, 1993) uniqueness lies in the fact that it chronicles the life of baymen. Baymen were the fishermen who were the mainstay of the coastal region's economy, and as fishing declined as a viable way to earn a living, longtime local residents feared the legends of the baymen would be lost.

So they created a museum, built as a replica of a "duck shanty", and filled it with local mementos, such as a "sneakbox"—a small sailboat that coasted virtually on top of the water, thus not warning waterfowl of its approach, clam rakes (the area was once a major source of clams and oysters), and of course, decoys. The decoy collection here is admittedly not as outstanding as that of the Ward Museum in Salisbury, Maryland (see page 49), but local carvers aren't afraid to hold their work up against better known carvers elsewhere.

Plans are already underway to create "Tuckerton Seaport" on an 11-acre site across the road and just north of the present museum. An enlarged museum (9,500 square feet compared to the present 1,200) will be the centerpiece of the project, built as a replica of the Tucker's Island lighthouse that collapsed in a storm in 1927. Twenty-one other buildings, all replicas of locally signficant structures, will occupy the site.

71

West Orange (Essex County)

Edison National Historic Site

Address: Main Street and Lakeside Avenue (zip 07052)
Phone: (201) 736-0550
Hours: daily 9 to 5 except New Year's, Thanksgiving, Christmas
Admission: age 17 and over $2.00
Handicapped access: Visitor center only fully accessible
Parking: free lot 1/2 block north on west side of Main Street;
free street parking, but spaces may be limited
Time needed: 1-1/2 hours

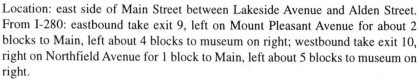

Location: east side of Main Street between Lakeside Avenue and Alden Street. From I-280: eastbound take exit 9, left on Mount Pleasant Avenue for about 2 blocks to Main, left about 4 blocks to museum on right; westbound take exit 10, right on Northfield Avenue for 1 block to Main, left about 5 blocks to museum on right.

Thomas Edison's laboratory is open by guided tour only, which includes his office-conference center-library, the main lab building, and the chemistry lab. Tours take about an hour and are offered from 10:30 to 3:30.

This was Edison's third research factory, built in 1887. By this time he was already well established as an inventor (the Menlo Park lab preceded this one) and this facility was built as an invention factory. However, some manufacturing buildings were also built, but it was clear that Edison spent most of his time in the labs and left his assistants to run the factories. Only a few of the buildings that once stood on the property remain. The lab remained in operation until after Edison's death in 1931.

The Visitor Center, starting point for tours, was the power house for the complex until about 1914. A small Edison museum is located here, but the real Edison is better seen in the tour of his office and chemical lab, where you'll get a glimpse into his character.

Edison held 1,093 patents, and many of his inventions are displayed: motion pictures, the storage battery (intended for electric cars, which were on their way out about the time the battery was perfected), the phonograph, among others. A replica of his movie studio, the "Black Maria", stands next to the physics lab. This was a rotating building to allow sunlight in.

Also available at no extra charge are guided tours of Edison's 23-acre estate *Glenmont* in nearby Llewellyn Park. These tours are given Wednesday through Sunday from 11 to 4 and last one-half hour. Glenmont is about 3/4 of a mile away, in a now, as in Edison's time, private residential area. Obtain tickets at the Visitor Center.

PENNSYLVANIA

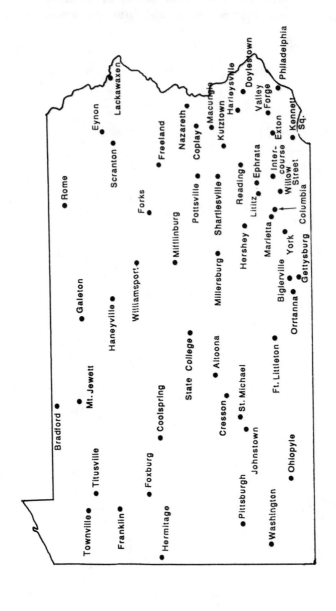

Altoona (Blair County)

Horseshoe Curve National Historic Landmark

Address: Burgoon Road (SR 4008) (mail to: 1300 Ninth Avenue, zip 16602)
Phone: (814) 946-0834
Hours: May-October:
daily 9:30 to 7; rest of
year Tuesday-Sunday 10
to 4:30
Admission: free;
funicular to track level
$1.50 round trip, under
age 3 free
Handicapped access:
fully accessible
Parking: free lot on premises

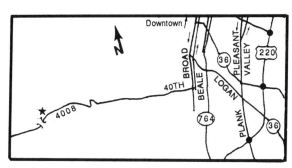

Time needed: 45 minutes to 1 hour
Location: 4 miles west of Altoona via 40th Street/Burgoon Road (SR 4008)

The famous Horseshoe Curve represented a major engineering advancement at the time of its opening in 1854. It has since been copied many times, but this is the only place in the U.S. where a museum has been built to celebrate the technology and construction of building railroads across mountains.

Allegheny Mountain stood as the most significant obstacle to the westward expansion of the Pennsylvania Railroad. The Pennsy's main competitor, the New York Central, had a water-level route from New York to Chicago and threatened the Pennsy's survival as a carrier from the East Coast to the burgeoning Midwest in the mid-1800s. But the Central's route was considerably longer, and the Pennsylvania could gain a big advantage if it could find a way over the mountain, which is, in this particular area, the eastern Continental Divide.

The Horseshoe Curve was designed by J. Edgar Thomson, the Pennsylvania's chief engineer. By building a wide-radius switchback, the grade could be reduced to 1.8 percent, a level that the locomotives of the day could manage. The museum exhibits tell the story of engineering and construction of the nearly half-mile long Curve, which was built entirely by hand. It is one of the most important developments of American westward expansion.

You can walk the 194 steps from the visitor center to the tracks, a 100-foot climb, or take the funicular (it runs every 5 minutes), to watch the numerous freights and occasional Amtrak passenger trains that pass every day. Other railroad memorabilia are on display, such as Pennsy dining car placesettings and menus, and operating HO-scale layouts depicting the Curve. Railroading souvenirs and books are on sale in the gift shop; its hours are 10 to 6:45 during the summer, but the same as the museum in winter.

The park surrounding the museum is a great picnic spot, overlooking a series of three reservoirs that hold Altoona's water supply.

Biglerville (Adams County)

National Apple Museum
Address: 154 West Hanover Street (zip 17307)
Phone: (717) 677-4556
Hours: April-October: Saturday and holidays 10 to 5, Sunday noon to 5; other times by appointment (call (717) 677-8728)
Admission: adults $2.00, children $1.00
(discount coupon page 157)
Handicapped access: fully accessible
Parking: free lot on premises
Time needed: about 1 hour
Location: south side of SR 394, 0.2 miles west of SR 34, 0.1 miles east of SR 234. Biglerville is 6 miles north of Gettysburg via SR 34.

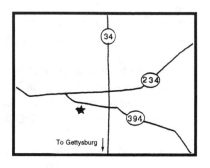

The world's only apple museum opened in 1990 in a Swiss bank barn built in 1857. Adams is Pennsylvania's leading apple growing county, with such well-known firms as Mott, Musselman, and Knouse Foods having processing plants nearby.

Begin with the 20-minute video on apple growing, a primarily promotional piece by the Pennsylvania apple trade association. A more technically oriented video on apple production is also shown on request. Then guides will take you on a 20-minute tour of the museum, following which you're free to look around on your own. There's a gift shop where you can buy apple-related products, both edible and non-edible. Tours to nearby apple farms and the Penn State experimental farm can be included by advance request.

As you enter, you'll see display cases filled with apple harvesting and production tools, and there are photos of a variety of apples grown in the area. The videos are shown in the auditorium to the left, which is also used for meetings, dances, and other local social functions.

The main museum is upstairs (handicapped access is via a ramp at ground level on the north side of the barn) and takes you from seed to cider, so to speak, in the process of apple harvesting. There are old plat plans of original settlers in the area, land indentures (some on sheepskin), crates stamped with the names of growers, a handmade 35-foot ladder for picking (called a "widow maker" for obvious reasons), tools such as sprayers, peelers, corers, and slicers, an 1863 cider press, a vinegar generator, a display case with mounted orchard insect pests, an apple butter kettle, and a simulated lab to check apples for acidity and firmness. A circa-1880 country kitchen and replica of Thomas' Country Store (a well-known business still operating at the town's main intersection) round out the exhibits.

There is a small library off the museum with books on apple production and local history. The library houses a rare 1858 Adams County map showing all property owners' names.

The final point on the tour is a free snack of apple juice and cookies.

Bradford (McKean County)

Zippo Family Store and Museum

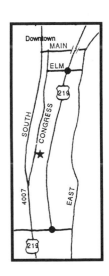

Address: Congress Street (mail to: 33 Barbour Street, zip 16701)
Phone: (814) 368-2863
Hours: daily 9 to 5 year-round, Saturday 9 to 2 except in winter
Admission: free
Handicapped access: fully accessible
Parking: free customer and visitor lot on premises
Time needed: about 1/2 hour
Location: east side of Congress Street just south of city line, 0.8 miles north of southern end of US 219 expressway via South Avenue (SR 4007)

Here's a museum that's definitely on the lighter side. Zippo started making lighters in Bradford in 1932. Over the years it expanded into other products: Case cutlery, tape measures, writing instruments, wood desk items, golf balls, and keyholders. Samples of the company's products are on display in the museum, but it's the lighters that make it unique.

The museum was developed in the company's retail store and opened on the 50th anniversary of D-Day, June 6, 1994. There are already plans to triple the exhibit space by taking over part of the warehouse to the rear of the building. A re-creation of the company's original plant, located on the second floor over a garage, is planned. Completion of the new museum is scheduled for July 1, 1995.

Zippo has always offered a lifetime guarantee with its lighters. If it can't be repaired, a new one is sent to the owner. The museum exhibits feature lighters damaged in use and returned to the company. The circumstances of the damage are grist for a museum's mill—for example, one was removed from the belly of a fish, others have been mangled by washing machines, run over by lawn mowers, or buried in mud. Some have saved the lives of soldiers by stopping bullets.

Also on display are specialty advertising lighters (one oversized one rode on top of a 1957 Oldsmobile), Vietnam era lighers, letters from soldiers serving in World War II, including one from famed correspondent Ernie Pyle. Pyle and Zippo founder George Blaisdell corresponded during the war, and through Pyle distributed lighters to GIs who coveted them because of their reliability. You'll also see photos of the manufacturing process from the 1940s to 1977, and the obligatory photos and newspaper articles chronicling the firm's history. There is also a video about the company and its products.

Although currently a small museum, pending completion of the expansion, but one that will "spark" your interest.

Columbia (Lancaster County)

Watch and Clock Museum
Address: 514 Poplar Street (zip 17512)
Phone: (717) 684-8261
Hours: Tuesday-Saturday 9 to 4 except holidays; also Sunday noon to 4 May-September
Admission: adults $3.00, seniors & AAA members $2.50, age 6-17 $1.00 (**discount coupon page 157**)

Handicapped access: fully accessible
Parking: free lot on premises
Time needed: 1 to 1-1/2 hours
Location: SE corner 5th and Poplar Streets, 1 block
north of SR 462 and 2 blocks east of SR 441. From
US 30 westbound, take SR 441 exit, go south on
441 (3rd Street) for 3 blocks, left on Poplar for 2
blocks. From US 30 eastbound, turn left at end of
exit ramp for 1/2 block, then right on 5th for 2
blocks to Poplar.

Time never stands still here at the headquarters of the National Association of Watch and Clock Collectors. Established in 1977, the museum has about 8,000 timepieces in its collection. The displays are true "timeshares"—they're changed periodically so all the pieces get exhibited in due course.

The tour begins even before you enter the building. There are three prominent clocks outside: a 70-foot tower housing a Howard tower clock movement (circa 1900) with Westminster chimes, a restored three-dial McClintock wall clock attached to the building, and a four-dial Seth Thomas street clock.

Once inside, you begin, appropriately, by punching the timecard you're given with your admission ticket in the antique time clock, then entering the museum proper. All varieties of American and European manufacture are displayed in a time-line effect, as well as photos and graphics describing methods of timekeeping in pre-Christian times. Each gallery covers a different period and nation, starting with the earliest timekeeping, then moving into the 17th century and on in some ten or so stages to the present. Each timepiece is identified by manufacturer, date, place, and, where appropriate, a description or history. There are inner workings shown for many different types and periods of timepieces, not just the outside faces, a fact which adds to the interest of the exhibits.

One of the most unusual pieces is Stephen Engle's monumental clock, completed in 1878 after about twenty years of work. It's immense—9 feet wide and 11 feet tall, and contains a clock, two organ movements, calendars, tide indications, a tellurian (an apparatus for showing how the earth's rotation causes day and night and seasonal changes), and many animated figures. This clock is the first such instrument in the United States and one of only about half a dozen ever made.

There are some special collections that are outstanding, such as Hamilton watches (made nearby in Lancaster), case clocks (mistakenly called grandfather clocks), and calendar clocks.

Not all watches and clocks are kept running, and in order to avoid the din if they all chimed at once, those that are running are set for different times. There are a few hands-on displays that describe how the pieces in question work. There are also some unusual designs, such as the weighted marble clock that drops a marble into descending rows calibrated in minutes, tens, and hours.

Even if timepieces aren't your passion, you're guaranteed not to get ticked off if you visit the Watch and Clock Museum.

Coolspring (Jefferson County)

Coolspring Power Museum

Address: Main Street (mail to: P.O. Box 19, zip 15730)
Phone: (814) 849-6883
Hours: April-October: 3rd Sunday 9 to 5; other times by appointment
Admission: June show $3.00, other times $2.00
Handicapped access: difficult due to grassy and gravel surfaces
Parking: free lot on premises
Time needed: about 1 hour, longer for shows
Location: just east of SR 36 on SR 3018, 9 miles south of Brookville, 10 miles north of Punxsutawney. From I-80, take exit 13 (eastbound-SR 36) or 14 (westbound-SR 28) into Brookville, then south on SR 36.

This museum, established in 1985, is dedicated to "restoring, operating, displaying, preserving, and interpreting historically significant and mechanically interesting early internal combustion engines". There are about 250 scattered about in twelve buildings as well as outdoors. Examples: four open-flame slide valve engines, oil field steam engines that were converted to gasoline power, and a 1912 National Transit engine used to pump oil. The oldest engine in the collection dates from 1879, the newest is pre-World War II. Many engines were manufactured in Pennsylvania to meet the needs of the steel, petroleum, and transportation industries. They were the primary supply of industrial power before electricity became dominant.

The engines were primarily put to industrial uses, but some saw marine and agricultural service. About 150 of the 250-plus engines are in working condition, a preservation effort which makes this the largest collection of operating internal combustion engines anywhere. Every engine is in its original state and has good identifying signs.

Dr. Paul Harvey, the director and tour guide, discusses the engines with a parent-like fondness and reverence. He says that as funds are available more buildings will be erected to shelter the machines from the weather. Right now only one of the twelve buildings is finished off and heated.

The museum puts on two shows a year, in June and October. The June show is larger and draws most of the museum's 8-10,000 annual visitors. The 1995 show will feature flame ignition/slide valve and pre-1900 gasoline engines, the largest such display ever put together. This is typical of the shows' themes; they're all run by volunteer members. In addition to the two shows, the museum publishes "Bores and Strokes", a once- or twice-a-year scholarly discussion of various types of historic engines.

Coplay (Lehigh County)

David O. Saylor Cement Industry Museum
Address: Saylor Park, 245 North Second Street (mail to: Lehigh County Historical Society, P.O. Box 1548, Allentown, PA 18105)
Phone: (610) 261-1200 or 435-4664
Hours: May-September: Saturday-
Sunday 1 to 4
Admission: free
Handicapped access: fully accessible
Parking: free lot on premises
Time needed: about 1 hour
Location: east side of 2nd Street, overlooking Lehigh River. From SR 145 (McArthur Road), go north from US 22 for 2.2 miles to Lehigh Street exit, turn right for 0.9 miles, left on Front Street for 1.3 miles to park on right. Front St. becomes 2nd St. in Coplay.

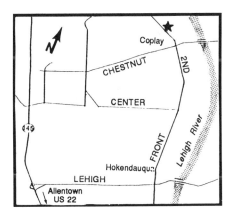

Guided tours trace the history of Portland cement making, born in the Lehigh Valley. Nine vertical kilns, built by the Coplay Cement Company in 1892, are standing on the site, which is owned and administered by the Lehigh County

81

Historical Society. It honors David O. Saylor (1827-1884), a Lehigh County native, considered the father of the Portland cement industry in America. The cement industry developed in this area because of the presence of abundant limestone and its proximity and rail access to major Eastern markets.

The vertical, or Schoefer, kilns here, developed in Germany, operated only until 1904, when rotary kilns had proven themselves much more efficient. The exhibits show the evolution of kilns, the founding and early history of Coplay Cement, a view of the interior of a kiln, tools and other equipment used in cement production, and steps in the manufacture of Portland cement. Historical scenes of local cement companies still operating are also on view.

The museum is undergoing renovation, but the exhibits are as described above. Future work will involve stabilizing the environmental conditions of the kilns.

Cresson (Cambria County)

Allegheny Portage National Historic Site
Address: US 22 (mail to: P.O. Box 189, zip 16630)
Phone: (814) 866-6150
Hours: daily 9 to 5 except Christmas
Admission: free
Handicapped access: fully accessible except spur trail to Skew Arch
Parking: free lot on premises
Time needed: 45 minutes to 1 hour
Location: 4 miles NE of town, 0.7 miles south of Gallitzin exit of US 22

This site commemorates the Allegheny Portage Railroad, the first step toward mechanized transportation over Allegheny Mountain prior to construction of the nearby Horseshoe Curve (see page 77).

The Allegheny Portage wasn't truly a railroad, although it did use locomotive power on level ground. It was a series of ten inclines in the 36 miles between Hollidaysburg, just south of Altoona, and Johnstown. At the time of its operation, 1834 to 1854, rivers and canals were the primary transportation mode across Pennsylvania. Hollidaysburg and Johnstown were the points where the streams became too steep for navigation, so the Portage lifted the canal boats in stages to succeedingly higher or lower elevations where water transportation could resume, at least for short distances, as would be the case with a normal canal. The ten inclines ranged in length from 1,480 to 3,117 feet, and lift varied from 131 to 308 feet. Total ascent was 1,398 feet on the eastern side and 1,172 feet on the western side. Stationery steam engines provided uphill power, and gravity downhill power on the inclines, with horses or steam locomotives on the levels.

A 20-minute movie describing the history of the Portage runs every half hour in the visitor center, and you can take a 2/3-mile round-trip walk to the foundation of Engine House 6 and the Lemon House, which had served as a tavern at the summit. The engine house's original foundation is enclosed within a reconstructed version that contains a working model of the steam engine used on the railroad. Tours of the Lemon House are given Saturday and Sunday at 1 and 3. A spur trail along the original right-of-way, though not handicapped-accessible, leads to the Skew Arch Bridge, which carried a wagon road over the railroad tracks.

Although this was not the only portage railroad in existence, it's the most famous, and the only one chronicled by a museum. This was truly a masterpiece of engineering in its day.

Doylestown (Bucks County)

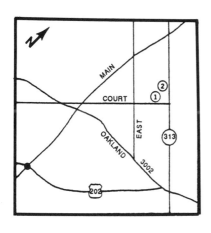

1   Fonthill Museum
2   Moravian Pottery and Tile Works

Fonthill Museum
Address: East Court Street (zip 18901)
Phone: (215) 348-9461
Hours: Monday-Saturday 10 to 5, Sunday noon to 5 except New Year's, Thanksgiving, Christmas. Reservations required for tours; last tour daily at 4.

Admission: adults $5.00, seniors $4.50, age 6-17 $1.50
Handicapped access: limited accessibility due to steps and narrow passageways—
call for details
Parking: free lot on premises
Time needed: 1 hour
Location: in Fonthill County Park, 1 mile NE of downtown; entrance also from SR
313 (Swamp Road) 0.2 miles north of Court Street

This unusual home—a castle, really—was built by and for Henry Chapman
Mercer (1856-1930), local Renaissance man, and is a National Historic Landmark.
But its uniqueness comes from its design and construction methods.

The house was built between 1908 and 1912, mainly to be a showplace
for Mercer's Moravian Pottery and Tile Works next door. The house was built
from the inside out, following the idea that "form follows function". It's of poured
concrete construction, highly unusual for a residence then or anytime, with literally thousands of inlaid tiles from his factory.

There are 44 rooms, 10 bathrooms, 18 fireplaces, and more than 200 windows. Despite the maze of hallways and staircases, no space was wasted. There
are no fewer than 11 different entrances and exits from the central hall. The house
had state-of-the-art conveniences for its day, including an elaborate heating system, dumbwaiters, an intercom buzzer system, and made maximum use of natural
light. The guided tour (there is a 12-person limit per tour) covers 14 of the rooms.
A photo book is available for the handicapped and persons not able to climb stairs
easily.

Some rooms, particularly the bedrooms, have built-in furniture such as
desks and chests. Mercer's factory produced the floor tiles used in the construction
of Pennsylvania's capitol building in 1906, which was the company's largest single
job. Some of the tiles in Mercer's bedroom are representatives of the Harrisburg
commission.

In addition to his own and foreign-made tiles, there are more than 900
prints collected by Mercer in his world travels as an archæologist and historian.
The inside of the house may strike some as cold and uninviting because of the
absence of carpeting and minimal artificial light, but in reality it's quite the opposite, as it exudes the breadth of knowledge of Henry Mercer.

Moravian Pottery and Tile Works

Address: 130 Swamp Road (zip 18901) (map page 83)
Phone: (215) 345-6722
Hours: daily except major holidays 10 to 4:45; last tour at 4
Admission: adults $2.50, seniors $2.00, age 7-17 $1.00, under 7 and Bucks Co.
seniors free
Handicapped access: first floor only
Parking: free lot on premises
Time needed: about 1 hour
Location: west side of SR 313 on NE side of town in Fonthill County Park, 0.2
miles north of Court Street, 1.1 miles north of US 202

Although the word "pottery" appears in its name, this facility is now, and has been for most of its existence, a tile factory. Another anomaly is that it has nothing to do with Moravians or the Moravian church, which established its first American roots not far away in the Bethlehem, Pennsylvania, area. It's just that Henry Mercer, the Bucks County-born world traveler and scholar, was impressed by Moravian stoveplate designs.

This National Historic Landmark was built in 1911-12 and operated until the mid-1950s. Tile making is still done, to produce inventory for the gift shop. There are about 300 different indoor decorative, not outdoor, tile designs always available for sale.

Tours of the factory start every half hour and are self-guided. You begin with a new introductory 15-minute video in one of the two most decorated rooms in the building. Tile making takes place on the first floor, but you'll go first up-stairs to see the ingredients. There are molds, tools (all described), cutters, the press area, kilns, original molds, and saggers. No, saggers are not employees who loaf on the job, they're containers that hold the tiles apart during the glazing pro-cess so they don't stick together. A hands-on mosaic activity area has been added to the tour in recent years. Each step in the process is covered.

Return to the first floor to see the original kilns close-up in the handpainting room, and the steps in firing and painting. These are the final stages in the produc-tion process. The tour ends in what was the company's office, next door to where you started. This is the other of the two most decorated rooms in the factory, boast-ing panels depicting the Fountain of Youth and the Columbus' departure from Europe and landing in the New World.

After visiting the Tile Works, and perhaps trying your hand at some of the steps in tile making, it's hard to leave without a souvenir from the gift shop.

Ephrata (Lancaster County)

Seiverling's Antique and Pedal Car Museum

Address: 66 Lancaster Avenue (mail to: 825 Martin Avenue, zip 17522)
Phone: (717) 733-1027
Hours: by appointment
Admission: free
Handicapped access: fully accessible via side entrance
Parking: free lot on premises
Time needed: 1/2 to 1 hour
Location: 1/2 block south of SR 272, 1 block east of US 322 interchange. Museum is second building west of Martin Avenue on north side of street.

I wrote in the Introduction that this book would not include antique car museums. True, there are a few antique cars here (outstanding specimens all), but the pièce de résistance is the pedal cars. This is perhaps the largest, or only, such museum in the country, and it's a well-kept secret.

Richard Seiverling, retired farmer and tractor salesman, started collecting pedal cars about 1991. He was already into the full-size versions, and you'll see those, but remember that you've really come to see the miniatures. There are over 60 of them and the number is still growing.

When he started acquiring pedal cars, Richard needed a place to keep them, so he built a one-story garage not far from his house. It's climate-controlled and so clean that you wouldn't mind undergoing surgery here. All the major pedal manufacturers are represented: Steelcraft, Murray, Midwest Industries, and others.

There's one instance of a pedal car and its adult equivalent parked side by side: dark blue '67 Mustangs (the big one is a model produced for export to Germany—only about 15 were made). Most of the kid-sized cars are from the late '30s to the late '50s, but a few are from outside that period. There's a rare '29 Lincoln and the aforementioned Mustang.

Not only are there cars, there's a '26 Mack Bulldog fire truck, a '52 Mercury police car with working siren and blue light, and a late '40s Jeep dump truck. Several cars have hoods or trunks that open and some have working headlights. All but three of the pedal cars have been restored, if that was necessary.

In case you're curious, pedal car collecting is not something you do with pocket change; cars have sold at auctions at prices exceeding those that the full-sized models brought when new.

Exton (Chester County)

Thomas Newcomen Library and Museum

Address: 412 Newcomen Road (zip 19341)
Phone: (610) 363-6600
Hours: Monday-Friday 9 to 5
Admission: adults $2.00, school age children 50¢
Handicapped access: not accessible due to steps
Parking: free but limited spaces on premises
Time needed: about 45 minutes
Location: east of SR 100, 1.5 miles north of US 30, 2 miles south of Turnpike exit 23. Turn east off SR 100 at Ship Road (SR 1001) traffic light, go 0.3 miles, left on Newcomen Road (SR 1025) for 0.4 miles to entrance on right.

Thomas Newcomen (1663-1729) developed the first successful atmospheric steam engine in England in 1712. Atmospheric engines used steam to create a vacuum which drives the pistons to produce power. His engine presaged the Industrial Revolution by harnessing steam power, whose benefits to manufacturing were already known, into a readily usable form.

The Newcomen Society of the United States, headquartered here, is a not-for-profit organization advocating free enterprise and the preservation of business history. The museum, the subject at hand, occupies one room in the main building on the property and displays samples of full-size steam engines and small scale working models of equipment powered by them. For the sake of convenience, the models now run on electricity, but all could operate by steam.

There are industrial, marine, and automotive engines, all of which operate by pushing a button on the side of the display cases. The highlights of the exhibit are a 1/24 scale of James Watt's double acting rotative beam engine of about 1788, mid-1800s table engines, single cylinder steam engine, and a tandem compound Corliss engine used around 1895 in a textile mill.

The museum recently opened the James Muldowney Printing Museum, which is, in reality, a working letter press shop. Jim Muldowney, now retired after about 40 years working at the Society, runs this operation. Although computers can now do much of the work performed here, Jim still sets type by hand and carves designs (mostly logos) onto blocks that go with the cold type in the printing process. There are drawers upon drawers of type and logo blocks that only Jim could find.

The Newcomen museum is a good place for children to learn the fundamentals of steam power by seeing it in a number of different applications.

Eynon (Lackawanna County)

Archbald Pothole State Park

Address: US 6 (mail to: Lackawanna State Park, RD 1, Box 251, Dalton, PA 18414)
Phone: (717) 945-3239
Hours: summer: daily 8 AM to 9 PM; rest of year 8 AM to sundown
Admission: free
Handicapped access: not accessible due to steps up to viewing platform
Parking: free lot on premises
Time needed: about 10 minutes
Location: east side of US 6, 1.1 miles east of SR 247, about 9 miles NE of Scranton

This is the world's largest and one of the finest examples of glacial potholes in the United States. It was discovered by coal miners in 1884 and is over 15,000 years old. The hole is from 24 to 42 feet in diameter at the top and 38 feet deep. Potholes are most often found on stream bottoms, where the erosive forces of water grind holes in underlying rock. They're deeper than wide and are common in areas that had been glaciated, as the northern half of Pennsylvania had.

Aside from its size, the pothole, showing the "polishing" effect of water wearing over thousands of years against the exposed rock, is exceptionally smooth.

It would be helpful to bring a flashlight, as there are no overhead lights illuminating the depths of the hole other than the sun. Since this is a state park, hiking and picnicking facilities are available.

Forks (Columbia County)

Twin Covered Bridges

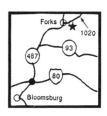

Address: SR 1020
Phone: none
Hours: daylight
Admission: free
Handicapped access: difficult due to uneven surfaces
Parking: free lot on premises
Time needed: 10 minutes
Location: 11 miles NE of Bloomsburg and 9 miles NE of I-80 exit 35 via SR 487; turn east at village of Forks on SR 1020 for 0.3 miles to park on right

Okay, covered bridges are not unique or unusual, at least not in Pennsylvania or in Columbia County, which has one of the greatest numbers of them in the state. But it's the only site, probably in the entire country, where there are tandem bridges. They were built in 1850 and preserved in 1962. The western bridge (closest to the road) crosses Huntington Creek, but the eastern span is over land, with a park beneath. During floods the eastern bridge likely also crosses water.

The bridges, although built at the same time, are not exactly alike. The western (longer) span has rainbow-shaped side beams which its partner lacks. However, in the overall world of covered bridges, one must say that both are rather ordinary looking. Oh, well, at least you can say you've seen them.

Fort Littleton (Fulton County)

Autos' Literature Shoppe and Museum

Address: US 522 (mail to: HCR 75, Box 238, zip 17223)
Phone: (717) 987-3702
Hours: Monday-Friday 9 to 5, Saturday 9 to 1
Admission: free
Handicapped access: difficult in gravel parking lot, a few steps inside to reach back of store
Parking: free lot on premises
Time needed: 20 to 30 minutes
Location: south side of US 522, 0.1 miles south of Turnpike exit 13

This combination store and museum deals in automotive memorabilia. If you owned, for example, a 1932 Hudson, you could probably find a repair manual for it here, or a cigarette lighter with the Hudson logo, or a set of playing cards with pictures of Hudsons on them.

That's the nature of this shop, started in 1974 and still owned by Paul Politis. There are cases and cases of accessories for old as well as newer cars. Shop manuals, owner's club magazines, posters, buttons, photo calendars, price books, keyholders, drinking glasses, anything imaginable or unimaginable made to advertise a particular make of car.

You're free to browse while the sales clerks take orders, mostly by phone from all over the country and beyond. Paul claims more than 1-1/2 million items in the 6,000-square-foot building.

If you're driving the Pennsylvania Turnpike and need a break, pull off at exit 13, turn left after you leave the toll booth, and you're practically at Autos' Literature's front door.

Foxburg (Clarion County)

American Golf Hall of Fame
Address: SR 58 (zip 16036)
Phone: (814) 659-3196
Hours: daily about 8 AM to twilight; inquire in advance in winter
Admission: free
Handicapped access: not accessible due to steps
Parking: free lot on premises
Time needed: 30 to 45 minutes
Location: top of hill at east end of town. Turn north off SR 58 onto Harvey Road for 0.4 miles to clubhouse on left. From I-80 exit 6, go south on SR 478 for 2 miles to SR 58 at St. Petersburg, turn right for 1.9 miles to Harvey Road on right.

The Foxburg Country Club is the site of the oldest golf course in continuous existence and at its original site in the United States, so it stands to reason that it should be the site of the American Golf Hall of Fame. The Golf House in Far Hills, New Jersey (see page 55) is larger, more contemporary, and more elaborate, but is not an official Hall of Fame.

How did golf in America originate in this isolated area? Joseph Mickle Fox of the Philadelphia area, whose family had a summer estate in Foxburg (any idea how Foxburg was named?), was introduced to golf at St. Andrews, Scotland in 1884. He returned with clubs and balls and began to play on the lawn of his estate. He soon built an 5-hole course and invited locals to play with him. Due to the boom created by the discovery of oil, northwestern Pennsylvania was loaded with wealthy people looking for leisure pursuits befitting their economic status.

Three years later a bigger course had to be built to accommodate the demand, and that is the 9-hole course used to this day. There are still sand boxes on every tee; these preceded the present-day tees invented in the 1920s. The present log club house was built in 1912. The 3-room Hall of Fame, chartered in 1954, is on the second floor and has just the kinds of artifacts you'd expect in a Hall of Fame. Of particular note is a set of clubs from each of six generations of the McEwan family, dating from 1770 to 1930.

The course is open to the public from April through October, but club members (there are now about 250 of them) may play year-round, conditions permitting. The club is mutually owned and dues are an astounding $300 a year.

Franklin (Venango County)

DeBence Antique Music World
Address: 1261 Liberty Street (zip 16323)
Phone: (814) 432-5668
Hours: Tuesday-Saturday 10 to 5, Sunday 12:30 to 5, closed New Year's, Thanksgiving, and Christmas
Admission: adults $6.00, seniors $5.00, children $3.00
Handicapped access: fully accessible except antique shop in basement
Parking: metered street parking and public lots nearby
Time needed: 45 minutes
Location: downtown, south side of Liberty Street (US 62/322-SR 8) between 12th and 13th Streets. From I-80 exit 3, go north on SR 8 for 15 miles to Franklin.

This "See and Hear Museum" opened in April, 1994, in a former G.C. Murphy store. From 1965 to 1992 Jacob and Elizabeth DeBence kept their music box and antique music machine collection in their barn a few miles outside of town. Following Jake's death in 1992, Elizabeth sold the collection to a group of local residents who, in order to keep it in the area, bought and renovated the then-vacant Murphy store. In the process they not only provided a more fitting home for this outstanding collection, they added a major attraction to the downtown business district, and thus spurred a noteworthy renaissance along the Victorian-era main street.

The museum's collection is extremely diverse, with about 125 working pieces on view. Here's just a sampling of the types of music boxes and machines: a ferris wheel auto phonograph, nickelodeon, orchestrion, traveling lap organ, symphonion, musette and cylinder record players. Some of these names are undoubtedly unfamiliar to you. An orchestrion looks like a piano, but is really an orchestra in itself. The 1912 Berry-Wood orchestrion was used in silent movie houses, and is thought to be the only one of its kind in existence. Numerous other pieces in the collection are similarly rare.

The museum's oldest piece is a cylinder box from Switzerland, circa 1870. Most of the other items date from the early 20th century. Volunteer guides will explain the pieces and play some of them for you. Even if you're not into old music-making machines, you'll enjoy hearing them, though not all at the same time. Despite being in a large room with high ceilings, the larger machines in action could blast you out of the place. A wide range of materials were used to make the "records". There are the commonly known paper piano rolls, wax cylinders and flat discs, but also more exotic perforated metal plates.

There are a few non-related antiques, such as mantle clocks, a high-wheel bicycle (called an "ordinary"), and lamps, but they are from the Victorian era. The store has been beautifully redecorated to the period with donated local labor. To help with expenses, the "bargain basement" is now an antique shop, open the same hours as the museum, where dealers rent spaces and run them as a regular shop.

DeBence Antique Music World is a tribute to what a committed community can do in recognizing and preserving a local treasure.

Freeland (Luzerne County)

Eckley Miners' Village
Address: SR 2051 (mail to: RR 2, Box 236, Weatherly, PA 18255)
Phone: (717) 636-2070
Hours: Monday-Saturday 9 to 5, Sunday noon to 5, closed holidays except Memorial, Independence, and Labor Days
Admission: adults $3.50, seniors $2.50, age 6-17 $1.50
Handicapped access: visitor center fully accessible; other buildings may not be accessible—call to discuss needs
Parking: free lot on premises
Time needed: 1-1/2 to 2 hours; 30 to 45 minutes for visitor center only

Location: 4 miles SE of Freeland off SR 940. Eastbound on SR 940 from Hazleton, bear right onto SR 2053 at Jeddo, go 1.8 miles, right on SR 2051 for 1.4 miles. Westbound, turn left off 940 onto SR 2053 for 1.7 miles, then straight onto 2051 for 1.4 miles. From I-80 westbound, take exit 40 and follow PA 940 west for about 7 miles to SR 2053. From I-80 eastbound, take exit 39, follow SR 309 south for about 2 miles to traffic light at SR 3022 (bottom of long hill). Turn left to Freeland, join SR 940 east for about 1 mile to SR 2053.

Eckley gained fame in 1968 as the locale for the movie "The Molly Maguires", an epic about the struggles of coal miners. It was a company "patch" town until 1971 when it was deeded to the state, whose Historical and Museum Commission now administers the property. Existing residents could remain, and now rent their homes from the state instead of from the coal company, but no newcomers have been allowed to move in. The population has gradually dwindled to about 16, but at its peak it was about 1,000.

The result of this preservation effort is an in-depth look at what life was like in a coal mining town from 1854 to 1970. The visitor's center houses exhibits of mining artifacts and family life, so begin there. You can also see a 15-minute video that describes a miner's work, his home life, and the village of Eckley (originally called Fillmore).

The visitor's center is open year-round, but guided tours of the out-buildings are offered from Memorial Day to Labor Day and on weekends in September and October. There are about 20 buildings lining the half-mile long main street, but only four are open with guide service. These are the Catholic church, built in 1862 and used until the early 1960s, the 1854 two-family miners' house, the company store built as a prop for the movie, and the Protestant Episcopal church dating from 1859. Some of the other buildings are under development and others are simply not open; the latter include the Sports and Social Club, the reconstructed (for the movie) mule barn and breaker, and a single-family home occupied by a foreman's or superintendent's family.

Mining here began underground, but in 1890 strip, or surface, mining took over, creating the scarred landscape and slag piles you see here and in many other parts of northeastern Pennsylvania's anthracite belt. Some surface mining continues just outside Eckley, but to see what an underground mine looks like, you'll have to go to Scranton (see page 138).

Although you can get a good overview of life in a mining town on your own here, having a guided tour of the outbuildings will give you a deeper understanding of the hard and dangerous life the miners faced.

Galeton (Potter County)

Pennsylvania Lumber Museum

Address: US 6 (mail to: P.O. Box K, zip 16922)
Phone: (814) 435-2652
Hours: Monday-Saturday 9 to 4:30, Sunday 10 to 4:30; closed weekends in winter and New Year's, Martin Luther King, Presidents, and Columbus Days and Thanksgiving and the day after and Christmas
Admission: adults $3.50, seniors $2.50, children $1.50
Handicapped access: fully accessible in visitor center, may be difficult in and around outbuildings due to uneven surfaces
Parking: free lot on premises
Time needed: about 1-1/2 hours
Location: north side of US 6 near top of Denton Hill, 11 miles east of Coudersport, 3.6 miles west of SR 449, 13 miles west of Galeton

The story of the lumber industry in 19th and early 20th century Pennsylvania is the subject of this museum, opened in 1972 and run by the state's Historical and Museum Commission.

Logging was the dominant industry in northern Pennsylvania in the late 1800s, and it's easy to see why. The thousands of square miles of forest that cover the area now were even even more abundant then. White pine, hemlock, and northern hardwoods were the prime varieties harvested.

A 12-minute slide show in the visitor center describes the history of lumbering in the region. There's an exhibit of a Depression-era CCC camp, of which there were many in the area, and another portraying lumbermen: their tools, the cutting process, log drives, and the leather tanning process (the connection between the lumber and leather industries is not well established by the exhibits). There are photos of Laquin, a now extinct lumber town located not far from the museum.

Taking the self-guided tour brochure, visit the nine outside buildings that would have formed a lumber camp: the bunkhouse-mess hall-kitchen, the blacksmith and carpenter shop, saw filer's shack, horses' stable, the engine house, laundry shed, loader shed, and sawmill. There's also a CCC cabin built in 1936 at a nearby camp and relocated here. Occupants of the CCC cabin were not lumbermen but unemployed young men for whom the Roosevelt administration created public works jobs during the Depression.

Lumbering is still alive in this area, but not nearly to the degree it was one hundred years ago.

Gettysburg (Adams County)

Cyclorama Center

Address: Taneytown Road (mail to: National Park Service, zip 17325)
Phone: (717) 334-1124
Hours: daily 9 to 5 except New Year's, Thanksgiving, Christmas
Admission: age 16 and over $2.00, seniors $1.50
Handicapped access: fully accessible
Parking: free lot on premises
Time needed: 1 hour
Location: south side of town in Gettysburg National Military Park, enter from Taneytown Road (SR 134) or Steinwehr Avenue (US Business 15)

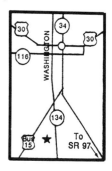

The Cyclorama is one of the most famous re-creations of the Battle of Gettysburg and one of only a few such works of art in the country. It was painted in 1883 by Paul Phillippoteaux, a French artist who came to the U.S. to study the battle and specifically Pickett's Charge. The circular painting is 356 by 26 feet and was brought to Gettysburg in 1913. As you view the painting a light and sound program recreates the Charge. Shows run every half hour between 9 and 4:30 and last 20 minutes. Be aware that there is no seating.

In the same building as the Cyclorama are newspaper and journal accounts of the Battle. Since this was before the days of on-site reporting, these are not eyewitness accounts, and so may not be entirely accurate. But that fact probably didn't matter much to a public hungry for news and unable to verify the accuracy of the reports.

There is also a copy of an 1871 painting of Gen. Longstreet's assault by Peter Rothermel (the original is in the State Museum in Harrisburg), and a display of items found on the Battlefield, a history of the Cyclorama, and antique maps,

95

paintings, and prints. Upstairs is a layout approximately 10 by 12 feet of the Gettysburg area with battle stations shown. Individual houses and buildings are shown, giving a very clear view of the stage set for the Battle.

The exhibits in Cyclorama Center are free; the charge is made only to view the Cyclorama itself. While you're here, take in the free 20-minute movie recounting the Battle in easily understandable terms. It's narrated by Richard Dreyfuss.

Haneyville (Lycoming County)

Fin, Fur, and Feather Wildlife Museum
Address: SR 44 (mail to: HCR 75, Box 25B, Lock Haven, PA 17745)
Phone: (717) 769-6482 or 769-6620
Hours: April-November: daily 9 to 5 (subject to change; call to confirm)
Admission: adults $5.00, age 12 and under $3.00 (**discount coupon page 157**)
Handicapped access: fully accessible
Parking: free lot on premises
Time needed: about 45 minutes
Location: east side of SR 44, 0.1 miles north of SR 664, 18 miles north of Lock Haven, 6 miles NW of Waterville, 33 miles NW of Williamsport

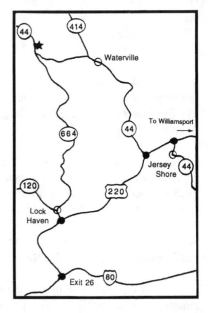

This is not your ordinary mounted animal museum. The 500-plus specimens on display here are nearly flawless representatives of their respective species. Many are the kinds of trophies game hunters only dream of capturing.

The museum was started in 1978 by owners Paul and Carole Asper. They have been hunting around the world since the early 1970s, and have the largest lifesize collection of sheep under one roof in the world, the "African Big Five" (lion, elephant, black rhinocerous, leopard, and cape buffalo), all spiral horned animals of Africa, including a bongo, a record Siberian elk, Persian brown bear, a two-ton Alaska walrus, and many North American animals. All specimens are identified as to name, country and date of kill. The mounts are grouped by continent.

96

During the course of your guided tour, you needn't worry about being bored to death with tales of how each animal was taken, unless you ask, and then you may only find out if Paul is there.

One of the museum's purposes is education, so there is a display showing how animals are fleshed out (they're skinned at the site, to reduce the weight that must be carried out of the field). There's a "touch and feel" table with skulls, animal heads, and an elephant's foot. Arrowheads and hunting artifacts are on display in the North American section.

Harleysville (Montgomery County)

Mennonite Heritage Center

Address: 565 Yoder Road (zip 19438)
Phone: (215) 256-3020
Hours: Tuesday-Friday 10 to 5, Saturday 10 to 2, Sunday 2 to 5; closed holidays
Admission: free; $2.00 donation suggested
Handicapped access: fully accessible
Parking: free lot on premises
Time needed: about 45 minutes

Location: east side of Yoder Road, 0.1 miles south of SR 113, 1/4 mile east of SR 63. From Turnpike exit 31, go north on SR 63 for 3.6 miles, turn right on SR 113.

This combination museum, library, and art gallery is the headquarters of the Eastern Mennonite Conference, the oversight body for Mennonite churches in eastern Pennsylvania, the oldest (but not the largest) of the group's settlements in North America. The Meetinghouse in which the Heritage Center is located is built in the style of a traditional Mennonite church building.

Mennonites are often confused with their offspring the Amish, a much smaller and stricter denomination. Mennonites do not shun all modern conveniences and freely mingle with the rest of society. Their mode of dress, while conservative, is not as plain and austere as that of the Amish. Mennonites are found all around the world and have an aggressive outreach program, both for proselytizing and for alleviating suffering among all religions and races.

Of particular interest to non-Mennonite visitors are the museum and gallery, where lifestyle items of church members are on display. There is a 20-minute video introducing Mennonite history from its European origins to the present. It's shown, appropriately, in a recreated meeting house of the late 19th century with its long pulpit and bench seats for the congregation.

A permanent exhibit, "Work and Hope", tells about the Mennonites' arrival in the Pennsylvania colony and their three centuries of life here. Other exhibits change about twice a year and cover subjects related to the sect.

A *fraktur* room displays a number of these handwritten family records from local families. Frakturs are colorful drawings originating in Germany combining births, baptisms, marriages, childbirths, and deaths on one large sheet resembling in a way a college diploma but with much more artistic flourishes. They are usually in German. Fraktur drawing died out over 100 years ago as more formal record-keeping by government became common.

Another room in the building is devoted to the display of art by local Mennonite artists; some of it is for sale. The library has over 10,000 books and documents relating to church history. A gift shop sells books, quilts, and religious items.

Hermitage (Mercer County)

Avenue of 444 Flags and Visitor Center
Address: 2634 East State Street (zip 16148)
Phone: (412) 346-0444
Hours: Avenue of Flags open 24 hours; call weekdays 8 to 4 to arrange guide service
Admission: Avenue of Flags free
Handicapped access: Avenue of Flags fully accessible
Parking: free spaces on premises
Time needed: Avenue of Flags 15 to 30 minutes
Location: just east of Sharon on north side of US Business 62. From I-80 exit 1, go north on SR 60 for 3/4 mile to SR 18 north, follow 18 for 3.3 miles to US Business 62 (0.3 miles past US 62), turn left for 1/2 mile to entrance to Hillcrest Memorial Park on right.

There are two parts to this unique place. The Avenue of 444 Flags is located in Hillcrest Memorial Park, a privately owned non-sectarian cemetery. The Visitor Center was located directly across the street, but is temporarily closed and may be relocated. Future plans will be announced, but no definite date has been set.

The Avenue was established to honor the 53 Americans held hostage by Iran from November 4, 1979, to January 20, 1981, a period of 444 days. Tom Flynn, owner of Hillcrest, started by erecting 100 flags on the hundredth day of the crisis and adding one a day until it ended. Most of the flagpoles have plaques indicating the honoree's name or that of the flag's sponsor.

Upon the installation of the 100th flag, the parents of Michael Matrinka, one of the hostages from Olyphant, Pennsylvania, lighted a flame that was to burn until all hostages were released. When that release occurred, Michael lighted the eternal flame with fire taken from the flame his parents had lighted almost a year earlier. The eternal flame stands in front of a monument erected to commemorate the failed rescue attempt in which eight Americans died.

The flags fly 24 hours (they're lighted at night), so they wear out and are replaced about every six months. Visitors' donations fund the purchase of replacements.

The Avenue is also unique among the places described in this book in that its attraction is psychological or emotional, not educational or visual. You don't come here for a scenic view (although the display is certainly attractive enough); you come for deeper contemplation.

Hershey (Dauphin County)

Chocolate World
Address: Park Boulevard (zip 17033)
Phone: (717) 534-4900
Hours: January-March: Monday-Saturday 9 to 4:45, Sunday noon to 4:45; April-mid-June: daily 9 to 4:45; mid-June-Labor Day: daily 9 to 6:45; Labor Day-mid-November: daily 9 to 4:45; special hours mid-November-December. Closed New Year's, Easter, Thanksgiving, Christmas
Admission: free
Handicapped access: fully accessible
Parking: lot adjoining property, up to 2 hours free
Time needed: 15 minutes
Location: on north side of Park Blvd. adjoining Hersheypark. From US 322 eastbound, take SR 39 exit and go east for 2.5 miles to traffic light where SR 39

turns left. Turn right for 1/2 mile to entrance on left. From the east via US 322 or US 422, turn right on SR 743 north, cross railroad bridge, then immediately turn left for 1/2 mile to entrance on right.

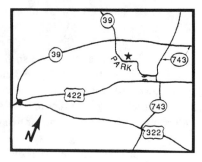

Chocolate World opened in 1973 as a replacement for the plant tour of Hershey Foods' main factory, and is a mechanized, "anti-septic" tram ride through the chocolate candy manufacturing process. The smell of chocolate pervades the air to create the "mood" as the tram twists and turns through a cleverly designed tunnel of lighted display windows that are mirrored to multiply the images. So instead of seeing one row of kisses going through the formation process, you see several.

As you enter, walk up a Z-shaped ramp past photographs and verbal accounts of the history of the company, the life of its founder, Milton S. Hershey, and his contributions to the community. Then you descend a stairway (check at the information desk inside the entrance for wheelchair access) to continuously running trams to start the 10-minute tour of what goes on in the plant located about a mile away. All the stages of manufacturing are depicted, with synchronized narrations on speakers on each tram. As you might expect, there's a commercial for Hershey chocolates at the end of the ride. Yes, there are free samples handed to you as you detrain.

You leave by another long sloping ramp that just happens to lead to the "Village of Shops" where you can succumb to the olfactory stimulation that has accompanied you throughout the tour. There's a café and specialty shops in addition to a place to contribute to Hershey Foods' bottom line.

Chocolate World might leave a bitter taste if you're a "techie" who likes to walk the shop floor and see the machines in action. But the by now nearly two million visitors a year would create a serious traffic jam and other possible hazards at the plant, so the tram tour is the next best thing.

Intercourse (Lancaster County)

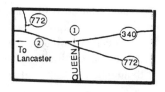

1   American Military Edged Weaponry Museum
2   People's Place Quilt Museum

American Military Edged Weaponry Museum

Address: 3562 Old Philadelphia Pike (mail to: P.O. Box 6, zip 17534)
Phone: (717) 768-7185
Hours: May-November: Monday-Saturday 10 to 5:30; March-April: Saturday 10-5:30
Admission: adults $3.00, under age 16 $1.50
Handicapped access: not accessible due to steps
Parking: free street parking; spaces could be limited in summer and fall weekends
Time needed: about 1/2 hour
Location: center of town where SR 340 and 772 eastbound diverge; 11 miles east of Lancaster

Located, fittingly, in a former bank, this museum houses, as its name implies, military knives, swords, and bayonets. With over 1,500 pieces on display, this is the world's largest such ollection. It covers the pre-Revolutionary War period to Operation Desert Storm. (A few pages ahead, you'll read about another edged weaponry museum, but that one differs significantly from this one, enough so that both have been included.) Recently, in the first departure from edged weapons, and in response to requests from visitors, owner Larry Thomas added about 30 military guns.

Displays are attractively arranged by subject and by period, with good explanations of the specimens. The museum's brochure provides a brief history of American military knives, and Larry will be only too happy to fill you in about the development and use of each specific group of pieces.

There's a gift shop here, but this is overwhelmingly a museum, not a sales facility. There are a few books on military weapons, along with some samples, but the availability of weapons varies.

People's Place Quilt Museum

Address: 3510 Old Philadelphia Pike (mail to: P.O. Box 419, zip 17534)
Phone: (717) 768-7171
Hours: Monday-Saturday 9 to 5
Admission: adults $4.00, under age 12 $2.00
Handicapped access: not accessible due to steps at entrance; museum on second floor
Parking: free street parking; spaces could be limited in summer and fall weekends
Time needed: 30 to 45 minutes
Location: center of town, south side of SR 340-772; 11 miles east of Lancaster

Quilts in recent years have grown beyond their utilitarian function into an increasingly popular art form. Many are made by Amish women, which accounts to some extent for the demand. The Quilt Museum displays a wide variety of quilts, with the exhibit changing about every six months. There are usually Amish-made quilts, but others get their turn as well. Around year-end the museum conducts a Christmas quilt challenge and displays the 38 finalists, which in 1994 came from 14 states and Canada. They ranged in size from 25 by 25 to 89 by 89 inches.

The museum occupies several rooms on the second floor above People's Place Country Store, a mecca for souvenir hunters visiting the Amish country. The museum portion has the distinct look of an art gallery, an effect which seems a little incongruous for the display of Amish-made quilts. The Amish are known for their use of simple designs, reflecting their un-modern way of life. Having their work displayed in a setting such as this hints unmistakably at commercialism.

But one cannot deny the beauty or quality of the work, and here, at least, you can examine the quilts in a quiet setting without pressure to buy. You can concentrate on the simple beauty they project.

Johnstown (Cambria County)

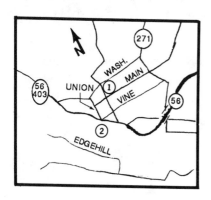

1   Johnstown Flood Museum
2   Inclined Plane

Johnstown Flood Museum

Address: 304 Washington Street (mail to: P.O. Box 1889, zip 15907)
Phone: (814) 539-1889; (800) 237-8590
Hours: May-October: Sunday-Thursday 10 to 5, Friday-Saturday 10 to 7; rest of year: daily 10 to 5

Admission: adults $4.00, seniors $3.25, age 6-18 $2.50
Handicapped access: fully accessible
Parking: metered street parking and public lots nearby
Time needed: about 1 hour
Location: downtown, SE corner of Washington and Walnut Streets

I thought long and hard about including this museum in the book. I had no doubts about its uniqueness, or, for that matter, its excellence, and surely you won't either. But applying the criteria I set forth in the Introduction, I could have excluded it with the rationale that it's based on a historical event. I finally decided that its uniqueness, as the only museum dedicated specifically to a flood, was sufficient to warrant including it.

The magnitude of the 1889 Johnstown flood is hard to contemplate, but after visiting the museum and seeing the Academy Award-winning documentary film, you'll have a better understanding of the destruction and the speed with which it took place.

Located in a landmark building that had been a Carnegie library, the museum was dedicated on May 31, 1989, the 100th anniversary of the flood. Its three floors of permanent and changing exhibits depict, using photos, displays of personal possessions found in the wreckage, maps, and a lighted diorama, the causes of the flood, the catastrophe itself, and the aftermath.

The best place to start is with the 15-minute video, shown hourly in the second-floor theater. Then return to the first floor to begin viewing the exhibits. One of the first displays you'll see is the lighted diorama showing the Little Conemaugh valley from above the South Fork Dam 14 miles downstream to Johnstown. There's also the list of the 2,209 victims extending along the wall. The personal effects of victims and moving and still videos of before and after are also among the permanent first floor displays.

Then move up to the third floor to view changing exhibits, which, while not all related to the flood, describe some aspect of the community, its industries, and people.

There's no doubt you'll leave this museum with a greater sense of awe over the destructive power of water.

Inclined Plane
Address: 711 Edgehill Drive (zip 15905)

103

Phone: (814) 536-1816
Hours: Monday-Thursday 6:30 AM to 10 PM, Friday-Saturday 6:30 AM to midnight, Sunday 9 AM to 10 PM
Admission: adults $2.00, age 5-16 $1.25—both fares are round trip; seniors free with ID during non-peak hours. Car and driver $3.00 one-way. Visitors center and observation deck free.
Handicapped access: fully accessible
Parking: free lots at bottom and top stations
Time needed: about 1 hour, including waiting time
Location: bottom station: downtown on SR 56-403 at Union and Vine Streets

This is the world's steepest inclined plane and the only one capable of carrying cars. At a grade of 71.9 degrees, it rises 500 feet in just 896 feet of travel. During the two-to-three-minute ride it's not hard to feel as if you're going to fall off the side of the hill.

The Incline, a National Historic Site, began operations in 1891 and carries an average of about 30,000 passengers a year. Most are visitors, but some are locals living on the top of the hill who use the Incline as a quick way to get downtown, as the driving route is much more circuitous.

Needless to say, the view from the top is magnificent. The city and the surrounding hills and valleys are spread out before you. Johnstown looks as if it was cloned from Pittsburgh (no, it's not the other way around—Pittsburgh is older). Consider these similarities: both have two rivers merging to form a third, which initially flows northwest from its source; both have compact, level central business districts in a triangle formed by the two merging rivers, with a steep hill forming the third side of the triangle; both cities were famous for steel production; both have a stadium at the junction of the rivers; both have disjointed and confusing street patterns outside of downtown because of the obstacles created by the hills; both have suffered numerous severe floods because of their topography; and both have inclined planes.

If you're a visitor to Johnstown, you're most likely to board the Incline at the bottom station. There are two samll parking areas on the west side of Route 56-403, one at the pedestrian entrance at the intersection of Union and Vine Streets, where there is a signal-controlled crosswalk to enable you to cross safely, and the other at the auto entrance a block farther north, opposite the intersection of Lincoln and Johns Streets. Plan to spend some time at the top, maybe even have a meal at the Incline Station Restaurant and Pub while you take in the view. There's an observation deck, visitors' center with exhibits pertaining to the Incline, and ice cream and gift shops. At night a spectacular laser light show creates sculptures in the sky, and you can't get a better view than from the observation deck.

Kennett Square (Chester County)

Mushroom Museum at Phillips Place
Address: US 1 (zip 19348)
Phone: (610) 388-6082
Hours: daily 10 to 6 except holidays
Admission: adults $1.25, seniors 75¢, age 7-12 50¢
Handicapped access: fully accessible
Parking: free lot on premises
Time needed: 15 to 30 minutes
Location: north side of US 1 at Orchard Avenue, 0.5 miles west of SR 52 at Longwood Gardens, 0.7 miles east of the east end of the US 1 expressway,

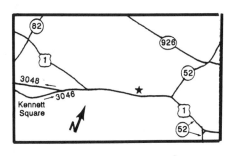

Southern Chester County is one of the nation's premier mushroom growing areas (although not the largest producing county in the state), so it's fitting that there be a museum here to commemorate that fact. This is a small museum (one room, entered through a gift shop), but, after all, mushrooms don't need a lot of space.

Lighted wall panels depict mushroom growing and harvesting, their origins, and the do's and don'ts of mushroom cultivating and eating. Another display answers the question "what is a mushroom?" There's also an 18-minute film on mushroom growing, and you'll see common and exotic mushrooms being grown.

Kutztown (Berks County)

Cut and Thrust Edged Weapons Museum
Address: 211 West Main Street (zip 19530)
Phone: (610) 683-5683

Hours: Saturday 9 to 5, Sunday noon to 5 year-round; Thursday-Friday noon to 5 added June-August
Admission: adults $3.00, seniors and students $1.50, refunded upon purchase (**discount coupon page 157**)
Handicapped access: not accessible due to steps
Parking: free 2-hour street parking, private lot in rear (enter via alley from side streets)
Time needed: about 1 hour
Location: downtown, north side of Main Street (old US 222) between Noble and White Oak Streets, 1-1/2 blocks west of SR 737

Like its counterpart the American Military Edged Weaponry Museum in Intercourse (see page 101), this relatively new museum (established 1990) is located in a former bank. But this one covers an earlier time period—the Middle Ages to about the American Revolution. Visiting one should not preclude seeing the other.

The rear of the first and second floors is a consignment gallery, with about 90 dealers having merchandise for sale; here the "inventory" is sometimes outside the museum's main subject matter. So we'll concentrate on the items on exhibit.

Most periods and most countries from the 15th to 18th centuries are represented in the first floor exhibits, which occupy what had been the banking floor and walk-in vault. You'll see armor, pole arms, swords, daggers, maces, and knives. Here are some of the rarities in the collection: Tom Thumb's sword, an Italian Gothic period (about 1510) suit of armor, fully movable (the technical term is "articulated"); a 1629 Couteaux de Breches carried by the elite guard of Ferdinand II; a small cannon from the Battle of Acre (1840) with 24-karat gold inlay and hand-carved tripod; a vampire killing kit commonly carried in Europe in the mid-1800s, especially if going to Transylvania (the crucifix in the kit has a hidden gun); a 1510 Swiss crossbow with 1,000 pounds pull on the bow; a Scottish *targe* from about 1690; and the armor worn by Charlton Heston in "Ben Hur".

Co-owner Ron Howell's prize possession, kept in a rotating plexiglas mount in the vault, is Gen. Lafayette's Revolutionary War sword given by him to Major John Lilly (later the first superintendent of West Point).

All the display items have identification cards, but Ron or his wife Lisa nonetheless conduct the tours, giving you much more information than you could glean from the cards. Without a doubt, this museum is a treasure trove of unique and unusual relics.

Lackawaxen (Pike County)

Roebling Bridge and Delaware Aqueduct

Address: mail to: National Park Service, P.O. Box C, Narrowsburg, NY 12764
Phone: (717) 685-4871
Hours: bridge open daily; tollhouse open weekends Memorial Day-Labor Day; call for exact hours
Admission: free
Handicapped access: bridge fully accessible, but not tollhouse due to steps
Parking: free adjacent lot on both sides of Delaware River
Time needed: bridge and tollhouse about 15 minutes each
Location: on Delaware River, 0.2 miles east of SR 590 in center of village, 20 miles NW of Milford via US 6, SR 434, and SR 590; 20 miles NW of Port Jervis, NY, via NY SR 97

This landmark was built in 1847-48 as an aqueduct on the Delaware and Hudson Canal and was later converted to a highway bridge. It's the only one of four D&H aqueducts still standing. It's also the oldest of John A. Roebling-designed bridges remaining and the oldest wire suspension bridge in the United States retaining its original principal design elements. While wooden parts of the bridge have been replaced, the original 1847 cables are still in place.

The purpose of the aqueduct was to provide a means of transporting loaded coal barges across the Delaware River without colliding with rafts of timber floating downstream. After railroads put the Canal out of business, the bridge was converted to vehicular use. The towpaths that were in use on the aqueduct were reconstructed in early 1995. The D&H Canal linked the gravity railroads north and west of here to the Hudson River near Kingston, New York, and provided a means of shipping anthracite coal from Pennsylvania mines to the port at New York City.

Since the building is not heated, the tollhouse exhibits, consistly mostly of photos and maps, are open only during the summer. They describe the canal system in general, and the D&H in particular, as well as John Roebling. There is a small book sales store in the tollhouse and nearby at the Zane Grey Museum in Lackawaxen, around the corner from the bridge.

Roebling (1806-1869) is most famous for designing and supervising construction of the Brooklyn Bridge, a project in which he lost his life. But he built other suspension bridges first, and this was one of his earliest. The bridge reopened for vehicular use in 1987, after being closed for several years, following rebuilding of the floor.

107

Lititz (Lancaster County)

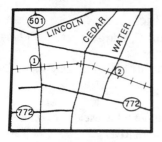

1 Candy Americana Museum
2 Heritage Map Museum

Candy Americana Museum

Address: 46 North Broad Street (zip 17543)
Phone: (717) 626-1131
Hours: Monday-Saturday 10 to 5
Admission: free
Handicapped access: not accessible due to steps to entrance
Parking: metered street parking and public lots nearby
Time needed: 30 to 45 minutes
Location: center of town on west side of SR 501, 1/2 block north of SR 772; 9 miles north of Lancaster

The Wilbur Chocolate Company has been making the sweet stuff for over 100 years, first in Philadelphia, and since 1930 in Lititz. They opened the museum in 1973 in two rooms behind the candy store. As at Hershey Foods, OSHA and FDA regulations have brought the demise of plant tours, so the museum helps fill the void. Sorry, no free samples.

There's all the hardware that goes into making chocolate: molds, wrappers, tin containers and the advertising that went on them as well as elsewhere. Of special note is the large collection of European chocolate pots, some of them hand-painted and over 200 years old. Hot chocolate was served in these in much the same way coffee or tea are now.

A circa-1900 candy kitchen with all the production equipment shows how candy was made almost a century ago. There are also vintage machines used in harvesting cocoa beans.

There's an "antique" feel to the museum; you know you've stepped into another era when you pass through the front sales room and into the exhibits. This is definitely not your modern, anti-septic factory tour.

Heritage Map Museum

Address: 55 North Water Street (zip 17543)
Phone: (717) 626-5002
Hours: Monday-Saturday 10 to 5
Admission: age 13 and over $4.50, seniors $4.25, age 6-12 $3.50
Handicapped access: not accessible due to steps to entrance
Parking: free lot on premises
Time needed: about 45 minutes
Location: 2 blocks east of center of town; turn north off Main Street (SR 772) onto North Water Street for 1/2 block to museum on right, just beyond railroad

This museum opened in May, 1994 in an old warehouse—a site well suited to its subject. Antique maps were first the hobby, now the vocation of Jim Hess, founder and curator. There are well over 200 maps on view, identified as to date, maker, and historical importance, and attractively mounted and displayed as if in an art gallery, which, in a sense, this is. They date from the 15th to 19th centuries and cover most of the U.S. states (some were the earliest maps made of the states after admission to the Union), European countries, the Middle East, and westward expansion to and within the U.S.

A sizeable part of the collection is of significant views of world events or locations and noted cartographers' works from around the world. Many of the maps are "firsts" of their kind, and reflect a surprisingly broad and accurate knowledge of their subject, given the poor communication and limited printing and reproduction capabilities of the 16th and 17th centuries. Some had drawings of native inhabitants accompanying the land, rivers, and roads.

Tours are mainly self-guided, but Jim does some escorting, and is happy to answer questions or detail the significance of any of the maps, from a historical or cartographic perspective. The gift shop in the large back room has several hundred additional maps, globes, and books on sale. The rare old maps for sale bring appropriately high prices, but you can start your own collection for a much more modest sum.

When you visit the Heritage Map Museum, you'll see not only the world (or state) as it existed at the time a map of it was drawn, you'll also get an insight to how the cartographer understood it and expressed it based on that perception.

Macungie (Lehigh County)

Allen Organ Company

Address: 300 West Main Street (zip 18062)
Phone: (610) 966-2202
Hours: by appointment only; call Monday-Friday 9 to 4
Admission: free
Handicapped access: fully accessible
Parking: free lot on premises
Time needed: 1/2 to 1 hour
Location: west edge of town on south side of SR 100; 9 miles SW of Allentown

This is Allen Organ's sales facility and is not run as a museum *per se*, but if you have a serious interest in organs, either as a prospective buyer, player, or historian, the company will be glad to show you its antique organ collection. The necessity of setting aside an employee's time is the reason for the requirement for an appointment, and you will probably be questioned about the level of your interest.

Allen is the largest church organ builder in the world, with 55 to 60 percent of the market, and the only true manufacturer (as opposed to assembler) of pipe organs in the United States. The firm makes about 20 different models at its two plants—one a short distance away in Macungie, and the other in Rocky Mount, North Carolina. The company prides itself on having replacement parts available for every Allen organ ever made.

The collection is in the Jerome Markowitz Memorial Center, built in 1991 and named for the firm's founder, who died later that year. There is a time line pointing out significant milestones in the company's history (it was founded in Allentown in 1937). A few highlights: it developed the world's first transistor organ (1959), the first electronic organ, the Lincoln Center (New York City) grand opening organ, and a computerized model in 1971 that was one of the first uses of digital technology. The oldest of the antique organs dates from 1803. Adjacent to the museum is a 400-seat auditorium where demonstrations are given using any of about half a dozen models.

Although not a traditional museum, a guided tour of Allen Organ's museum (which includes the sales floor) should strike a pleasant chord.

110

Marietta (Lancaster County)

Le Petit Museum of Musical Boxes

Address: 255 West Market Street (mail to: P.O. Box 135, zip 17547)
Phone: (717) 426-1154
Hours: March-December: Monday, Saturday 10 to 4, Sunday noon to 4, and by appointment
Admission: $3.00
Handicapped access: not accessible due to steps to entrance and crowded conditions inside
Parking: free street parking
Time needed: 1/2 hour
Location: south side of West Market Street between Gay and Perry Streets; 15 miles west of Lancaster via SR 23 or US 30 and SR 441

This small museum, located in a Federal-era townhouse, opened in January, 1994. It showcases only music boxes; there are about 75 of them, dating from 1820 to about 1900.

Most of the boxes are European, primarily Swiss, but there are examples of American manufacturers as well. The oldest is a tiny snuff box from 1820. You'll also see Swiss cylinder boxes, German disc type players, a Swiss Edelweiss box inside a photo album, a musical alarm clock, and the first U.S. juke box (1889). There's even a coin-operated musical birdcage. Most of the boxes are hand size, but there are some table and floor models. One example of the latter is the prize Regina (this company now makes vacuum cleaners) disc box from about 1895. The main feature of most of the boxes is their small size—some are little larger than a cigarette pack.

Owners George Haddad and David Thompson conduct the tours personally, and do small restoring jobs for other owners. You might be surprised to learn that music boxes are still being made; you can buy one in the small sales area in what had been the kitchen.

In addition to the music boxes, the ground floor of the home is filled with other types of antiques, but they're not for sale. In fact, they're the subject of changing monthly displays. The antiques are part of George's and David's collection and are here to enhance the "atmosphere" of the music boxes. A lot of Victoriana has been crowded into the four rooms, kitchen, and entrance hall comprising the museum. When you visit, please watch your step—very little space is unoccupied.

Mifflinburg (Union County)

Mifflinburg Buggy Museum
Address: 523 Green Street (zip 17844)
Phone: (717) 966-0233
Hours: May-mid-September: Thursday-Sunday 1 to 5; other times by appointment
Admission: adults $4.00, age 12-17 $1.50, age 6-11 50¢
Handicapped access: not accessible due to steps
Parking: free lot behind museum (enter via alley) and street parking
Time needed: 1-1/2 hours
Location: south side of Green Street between 5th and 6th; 2 blocks south of SR 45 (Chestnut St.), 1-1/2 blocks west of SR 304 (4th St.), 4-1/2 blocks east of SR 104 (10th St.)

One hundred years ago, Mifflinburg was the Detroit of buggy manufacturing, with numerous coachmakers in the immediate area. Despite the presence of a large Amish community nearby who still uses these conveyances, buggy production ceased by about 1930.

The William A. Heiss Coach Works operated for about 50 years until 1927 and consisted of three buildings to the rear of the Heiss family's home. The carriage house is a re-creation; the original burned down in the 1940s, but the other two buildings are original. In fact, the factory was left untouched from the time it closed until the Buggy Museum was founded in 1978. It's as if Mr. Heiss finished his day's work, intending to come back tomorrow, but never did. According to volunteer tour guide Margaret Gast, it's one of only six industrial museums east of the Mississippi that was never dismantled.

The house is also pretty much as the family left it. The two sons of William Heiss did not sell the house after their mother died in 1943 even though they weren't living in it. The house and factory are now on the National Register of Historic Places.

You'll tour the two-story house first, then move on to the workshop, a weathered two-story frame building. Construction took place on the first floor and finishing—painting, detailing (yes, there was pinstriping even then), seat upholstering—was done on the second. The original forge, hand tools, wheel-making machine, and gas-powered engine with belts and pulleys to run the equipment are all there. There was a blacksmith shop in the factory to shape and apply the metal "tread" to the wooden wheels. A wooden ramp was built to the second floor to move carriages to and from the shop via the alley.

Across the alley from the shop is the repository building, built in 1895 as a "showroom". There are about ten buggies of various types on display here, not all made by Heiss but most made locally.

As you return to the home, which houses a small gift shop, you'll see a board holding metal tags. These were the nameplates of buggy repairers, not the original manufacturer. The repairers would remove the builder's plate and replace it with their own, a practice that today would create considerable work for the legal profession.

The only thing missing from the museum is a buggy ride, but for obvious reasons that's not practical. But if you toured an auto manufacturing plant, you wouldn't get a test ride, either.

Millersburg (Dauphin County)

Millersburg Ferry

Address: foot of North Street (mail to: Millersburg Ferry Boat Association, P.O. Box 93, zip 17061)
Phone: (717) 692-2442
Hours: daylight from early spring to late fall, depending on river conditions
Admission: cars $3.50, motorcycles $2.00, bicycles $1.00, pedestrians 50¢
Handicapped access: accessible except for possible difficulty on ramps
Parking: free lot on premises at west dock, free street parking at east dock
Time needed: 1/2 hour plus waiting time
Location: Millersburg: turn west off SR 147 on North Street, 2 blocks north of US 209; west shore: turn east off US 11-15 at SR 34 intersection, 2 miles south of Liverpool, 10 miles north of US 22-322

The Millersburg Ferry is the only wooden stern paddlewheel ferry operating in the United States, and is the only ferry on the 444-mile Susquehanna, the longest river in the northeastern U.S. It's been in operation since 1825 on the mile-wide river.

Boats were poled by human power until 1873, when the first steam-powered paddlewheeler was acquired. Gasoline replaced steam as the power source in the 1920s and the paddlewheel was shifted to the stern (that's the rear for the nautically unscholared).

The ferry has had a number of owners in its 170-year history, but in 1990 was bought by a Millersburg bank and given to the Chamber of Commerce, which chartered the Ferry Boat Association.

The craft looks like something out of "Huckleberry Finn". The engine cabin and passenger seating room rest atop a barge-shaped platform, with the vehicle carrier literally strapped to one side.

A ride on the Millersburg ferry is a 30-minute step back in time—it's completely low-tech. It runs on demand and remains berthed on whichever side the last customers disembarked. Although the river is a mile wide, the operators will spot your car on the ramp and come for you. If you're on foot or bicycle, you'll probably have to wait until a larger vehicle arrives to catch their attention. At one time, there was a large white wooden board attached to a tree on the west bank, which you turned to face east in order to call the ferry.

The Susquehanna is one of the prettiest big rivers in America, particularly as it meanders through the scenic Appalachian ridge and valley section of Pennsylvania. There's no better way to enjoy the river's beauty than on the Millersburg ferry.

Mount Jewett (McKean County)

Kinzua Bridge State Park
Address: SR 3011 (mail to: c/o Bendigo State Park, P.O. Box A, Johnsonburg, PA 15845)
Phone: (814) 778-6118 or (814) 965-2646
Hours: daylight
Admission: free
Handicapped access: fully accessible
Parking: free lot on premises
Time needed: about 1/2 hour
Location: NE of town. Turn north off US 6

onto SR 3011 for 3 miles to entrance on left. From SR 59 at Ormsby, turn south on SR 3011 for 5 miles to entrance on right.

Like far too many places, the Kinzua Viaduct has been called the "eighth wonder of the world". But even a more objective observer would agree that this magnificent trestle qualifies as unusual, if not unique, and is definitely worth seeing. It's on the National Registers of Historic Places and of Historic Civil Engineering Landmarks.

It stands 301 feet above Kinzua (pronounced KIN-ZOO) Creek on top of the Allegheny plateau, at an elevation of about 2,200 feet. The viaduct was built in 1882 and at that time was the highest railroad bridge in the world. It is believed today to be the second highest in the U.S. and fourth highest in the world. It was originally constructed of wrought iron but was replaced in 1900 by a steel structure to better withstand the strong winds in the valley and to accommodate heavier trains.

The bridge is 2,053 feet long and as part of the Baltimore & Ohio Railroad carried regular freight trains until 1982. You can once again cross the span by train on excursions run by the Knox, Kane, Kinzua Railroad. Trains depart from Marienville (96-mile round trip) and Kane (32-mile round trip) on weekends from June to October, with weekday trips (except Monday) in July and August, and Wednesday through Sunday trips during the first two weeks in October. Contact the Railroad at P.O. Box 422, Marienville, PA 16239, or call (814) 927-6621. The bridge is also open for hiking and is wheelchair-accessible, but if you're acrophobic, you probably should enjoy the view from the overlook.

The Kinzua Viaduct is truly an awesome structure because of its immensity.

Nazareth (Northampton County)

C.F. Martin Guitar Company
Address: 510 Sycamore Street (zip 18064)
Phone: (610) 759-2837
Hours: Monday-Friday 8 to 4 except holidays; plant tours at 1:15
Admission: free
Handicapped access: fully accessible
Parking: free lot on premises
Time needed: about 1-1/2 hours for museum and tour
Location: just north of town. Go north on Broad Street (SR 4025) from SR 191 for 0.8 miles to Beil Avenue, right for 1 block to Sycamore, right to parking lot.

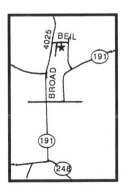

The Martin Guitar Company has been making guitars by hand since 1833, for all but the first six of those years in Nazareth. Its one-room museum display of vintage Martin instruments is a primary interest for musicians, while the main attraction is the thorough guided tour of the manufacturing facility.

C.F. Martin was born in Germany in 1796 into a long line of guitar and violin makers and came to America in 1833 to pursue has craft. He started in New York City but within a few years had moved to Nazareth, in an area of Pennsylvania not too dissimilar to their homeland. The company is now in the hands of the sixth generation of Martins. The present factory was built in 1964, after the manufacturer outgrew the 105-year-old factory in town that now serves as a company warehouse.

The factory tour moves through each step of a guitar's construction: from the shaping and joining of the sides to the fitting of the top and back, the fitting of the neck, and the finishing, buffing, stringing, and final inspection. What you see in one hour takes two to three months and involves over 300 separate operations. Obviously, one of the steps is waiting, while shaped wood cures, glues harden, and stains and lacquers dry.

Martin also makes mandolins, ukeleles, and banjos. If, after taking the plant tour, you want to order a guitar, you'll have to contact your local dealer; the firm does not sell direct. But you can buy supplies (picks, strings, and the like), as well as guitar memorabilia, in the 1833 Shop.

Ohiopyle (Fayette County)

Fallingwater

Address: SR 381 (mail to: P.O. Box R, Mill Run, PA 15464, or Western Pennsylvania Conservancy, 316 4th Ave., Pittsburgh, PA 15222)
Phone: (412) 329-8501
Hours: April 1-November 15: daily except Monday 10 to 4; rest of year weekends only and Martin Luther King and Presidents Days, the day after Thanksgiving, and the week between Christmas and New Year's
Admission: Tuesday-Friday $6.00, weekends $10.00; grounds and exterior only $3.00
Handicapped access: pavilion and first floor fully accessible, upper floors not accessible due to steps (video available)
Parking: free lot on premises
Time needed: 1-1/4 hours plus waiting time

Location: west side of SR 381, 3.3 miles north of Youghiogheny River bridge at Ohiopyle; 21 miles south of Turnpike exit 9 via SR 31 and 381, 10 miles north of US 40 via SR 381

Fallingwater is one of architect Frank Lloyd Wright's most famous designs and is unique in the way that it blends into its surroundings.

The famous house, built in 1936-38 as a retreat for the Kaufmann family of Pittsburgh department store fame, is now owned by the Western Pennsylvania Conservancy. The house can be seen only by guided tour lasting 45 minutes. Children under age 9 are not allowed; there is supervised child care center for $2.00 per child per hour. The tour is not advised for people with difficulty climbing stairs. Photography indoors is not permitted except on the 2-hour in-depth tour daily at 8:30 (advance reservations only), where still photos are allowed.

The house and its furnishings are as the Kaufmann family left them when son Edgar, Jr., donated the property to the Conservancy in 1963. Tours began the following year.

Rather than building the house to face the waterfall on Bear Run, as the Kaufmanns originally envisioned, Wright built it directly over the falls and cantilevered it on several levels into the rocky sides of the hill. The house, in effect, cascades off the cliffs just as the waterfall does. Construction is of native Pottsville sandstone, poured reinforced concrete, steel, and glass. It has a southern exposure to take maximum advantage of light and warmth. The house has been called the "quintessential Wright" and "the best all-time work of American architecture".

It's not an exceptionally large house—about 2,800 square feet—but most of the space is common, in that it was designed to be used for socializing by the family and their guests. The main house has only two bedrooms. The six outdoor terraces have almost the same square footage as the interior. Later, a separate guest house (essentially an apartment) was built. Wright designed the interior furnishings as well, making them fit the space.

Tour tickets are sold at the Visitors Pavilion, which also houses a gift shop, café, and exhibits pertaining to the house. The interpretative nature trail starts here. There are frequently waits for tours, especially on weekends, unless you have a reservation.

Orrtanna (Adams County)

Mister Ed's Elephant Museum

Address: 6019 Chambersburg Road (zip 17353)
Phone: (717) 352-3792
Hours: daily 10 to 5, 8 PM close Friday-Sunday in summer
Admission: free
Handicapped access: accessible, but with some difficulty in gravel parking lot and on narrow wooden ramp to entrance
Parking: free lot on premises
Time needed: 20 to 30 minutes
Location: north side US 30, 0.1 miles west of SR 234; 12 miles west of Gettysburg, 13 miles east of Chambersburg

Ed Gotwalt collects elephants, and he has about 5,000 of them on display here. The live variety is about the only type missing. He started collecting when he got an elephant as a wedding gift, but he has always had an interest in the giant pachyderms. You can thank Mrs. Ed for the museum's existence; before it opened about ten years ago, the collection was in their home.

Here's a sampling of the uses to which the elephants on view have been put: jewelry, bookends, candy dish, ink blotter, toothpick holder, Japanese tea set, clock, even a hair dryer and potty chair. They're made of glass, china, ceramic, brass, celluloid, wood, and fur. Ed stresses that he has nothing made of ivory from elephants' tusks.

The museum is located in a candy store, and of course you must pass its temptations to get to the museum. None of the elephants in the museum is for sale, but there are some in the store. Ed says that 95 percent of his visitors collect elephants or know someone who does. Even if you don't, you be entertained and amused by the contents of his museum.

Philadelphia (Philadelphia County)

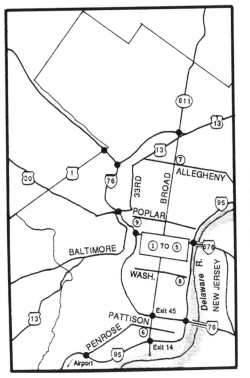

1 Afro-American Historical and Cultural Museum
2 Fabric Workshop and Museum
3 Mütter Museum
4 Polish-American Cultural Center
5 Shoe Museum
6 American Swedish Historical Museum
7 Historical Dental Museum
8 Mummers Museum
9 Neon Museum of Philadelphia

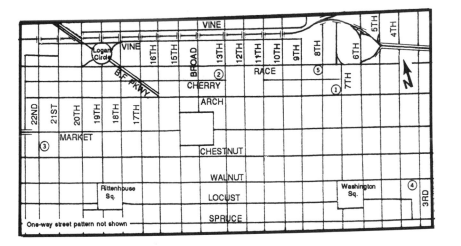

Afro-American Historical and Cultural Museum

Address: 701 Arch Street (zip 19106) (map page 119)
Phone: (215) 574-0380
Hours: Tuesday-Saturday 10 to 5, Sunday noon to 6 except holidays
Admission: adults $4.00, children, seniors, handicapped, students with ID $2.00
Handicapped access: fully accessible
Parking: metered street parking and public garages nearby
Time needed: about 45 minutes
Location: NW corner of 7th and Arch Streets. Subway (Market-Frankford and Broad St. lines) to Market East (8th & Market), walk east 1 block to 7th, left 1 block to Arch.

This museum was built by the city of Philadelphia in 1976 to show and interpret, as the name indicates, the history and culture of African-Americans. There are usually two changing exhibits.

Currently on display are "Design Diaspora", occupying the first and second floor galleries. This exhibit honors black architects and international architecture in general from 1970 to 1990. About fifty architects are honored, with some thirty paintings and models of their projects. The third and fourth floors are devoted (through December, 1996) to a primarily locally oriented exhibit "Healing the Body and Mind: the African-American Sports Tradition in Philadelphia". Photos of noted locally-born black athletes and professionals born elsewhere who played for local teams are also on display.

The museum occupies a modern concrete block and glass building with spacious exhibit space and spiral staircases between floors (elevators are also available). There is a gift shop just inside the entrance selling African-oriented jewelry, prints, posters, books, and other items.

American Swedish Historical Museum

Address: 1900 Pattison Avenue (zip 19145) (map page 119)
Phone: (215) 389-1776
Hours: Tuesday-Friday 10 to 4, Saturday-Sunday noon to 4, closed holidays
Admission: adults $4.00, seniors and students $2.00, under 12 free
Handicapped access: not accessible due to steps
Parking: free lot on premises (enter through F.D. Roosevelt Park)
Time needed: 1 hour
Location: south side of Pattison Avenue between Broad and 20th Streets in South Philadelphia. Subway (Broad St. line) to Pattison (last stop), walk west 1/2 mile on

Pattison. From I-76 (Schuylkill Expwy./Walt Whitman Bridge) take exit 45, go south on Broad St. for 1/2 mile, right on Pattison for 1/2 mile. From I-95 (Delaware Expwy.), take exit 14, go north on Broad for 1/2 mile, left on Pattison for 1/2 mile.

This is the oldest Swedish museum in the U.S., founded in 1926, located on land that belonged to a Swedish settler at the time of the New Sweden colony (1638-1655). This building opened in 1938 and is modeled after a 17th century Swedish manor house, Eriksberg. It's even more attractive inside than outside. As you enter, note the ceiling mural in the entrance hall depicting the arrival of the Swedes in 1638.

There are twelve exhibit galleries on the two floors. Each gallery concentrates on a separate subject relating to Swedish culture and Swedish-American history. The first floor in general deals with historical subjects, such as the New Sweden colony and Swedish immigration between 1840 and 1920, when one-fourth of the country's population came to the US. The first floor includes the Nord Library containing 20,000 volumes on Swedish and Swedish-American history. There is also a *stuga*, a Swedish farmhouse interior with traditional furnishings and costumes.

The second-floor rooms are devoted to decorative arts, textiles, paintings, engravings, Swedish women's accomplishments, Swedish architecture, and more recent artistic and cultural contributions of Swedes and Americans of Swedish descent. The rooms have art deco and modern motifs. One room features an exhibition on operatic singer Jenny Lind ("the Swedish nightingale"), another has an interpretation of the life of Fredrika Bremer, a 19th-century author, activist, and world traveler. Two rooms named for John Ericsson, an inventor and designer. A number of his inventions are shown, including his twin-screw propeller, solar engine, and the Civil War battleship *U.S.S. Monitor*.

The decor of the exhibit rooms is as evocative of Sweden as the displays themselves. In the Colonial Room, the walls and trim evince the colors of the Swedish flag. John Ericsson Room I has an art deco decor. The library has Swedish-made furniture and fixtures and is made of dark lacquered birch. Throughout the halls and the second-floor balcony are paintings and sculptures by Swedish and Swedish-American artists.

Fabric Workshop and Museum
Address: 1315 Cherry Street (zip 19107) (map page 119)
Phone: (215) 922-7303

121

Hours: Monday-Friday 9 to 6, Saturday noon to 4
Admission: free
Handicapped access: not accessible due to steps to building entrance
Parking: limited metered street parking; public garages and lots nearby
Time needed: about 1/2 hour
Location: NE corner of Juniper Street, between 13th and Broad. Subway (Market-Frankford line) to 13th & Market, walk north 1-1/2 blocks on 13th, left for 1/4 block on Cherry; or Broad St. line to Race & Vine, walk south on Broad 1/2 block, left on Cherry for 3/4 block.

This museum is likely to be very different from what you anticipated from its name. It's primarily a workshop that has exhibit space. Although it gets many visitors, it's not set up like a museum or to accommodate the typical comings and goings of museum visitors. In fact, you have to buzz to enter the building, then take the elevator to the fifth floor. There is no exterior signage for the Fabric Workshop and Museum except a small nametag on the buzzer. See, I told you it was different. Unique and unusual are most appropriate adjectives for this place!

The prime emphasis is on experimental design and production, with much less on display, of a wide variety of designs on textiles. Designs created here are printed on all kinds of materials: pillows, umbrellas, posters, shirts, in short, any kind of fabric that can accept a printed design. Designs run the gamut from functional to elaborate to indescribable. One might describe this as a working gallery, but in fact it's more like a working laboratory. It's the only non-profit organization in the country devoted to experimental fabric design and printing.

The workshop occupies the entire fifth floor of this older office-ware-house-type building. It's a single open space except for the elevator and stairway shafts and a fairly small exhibit area and even smaller gift shop that have been partitioned. The eastern side of the floor is the workshop area, with long tables where designs are drawn and then printed onto fabric in a process similar to silkscreening. The exhibit area is on the western side where artists-in-residence display their work. The exhibit, therefore, is constantly changing, and there are no permanent displays. Most of the artists' work is exhibited elsewhere. The gift shop sells what the Workshop makes, or adaptations of same, so its wares are as unconventional as the designs the artists produce.

The Fabric Workshop and Museum has been in existence since 1977 and has been very successful in furthering the careers of its emerging artists as well as those of established artists-in-residence.

Historical Dental Museum

Address: 3223 North Broad Street (zip 19140) (map page 119)
Phone: (215) 707-2816
Hours: by appointment only Monday-Friday 9 to 4
Admission: free
Handicapped access: building is fully accessible but access inside museum may be difficult due to narrow doorways and crowded conditions
Parking: metered street parking and private lots nearby
Time needed: 1/2 to 1 hour
Location: at Temple University School of Dentistry, east side of Broad Street between Allegheny Avenue and Westmoreland Street in North Philadelphia. Subway (Broad St. line) to Allegheny, walk north about 100 feet to entrance.

It may seem like pulling teeth to get to this place, but like going to the dentist, you feel better after you've been there.

Temple's School of Dentistry is the second oldest in the country, founded as the Philadelphia Dental College in 1863. It's been here, in what had been a Packard automobile factory, since 1947 (it's still called the Packard Building). The museum is on the fourth floor at the north end of the building. The entrance is via the newer portion, closer to Allegheny Avenue. Plans are to expand on the third floor of the new building, as some of the museums contents are in display cases in the fourth floor hall.

Susan Howell, the museum's curator since 1987, delights in havng visitors, but since she has another function as Director of Technical Support Services for the School, you have to call in advance for an appointment.

What will you see when you get here? How 'bout the first known dental chair in the United States, or an elephant's tooth, or a bucket filled with thousands of teeth pulled by Temple grad Edgar "Painless" Parker? Parker is not regarded as one of Temple's more illustrious graduates, at least by Temple. He advanced his career by blatant advertising, a habit inimical to the conventions of the day. In his years of practice he pulled thousands of teeth and evidently saved every one. Those not put to some ornamental use were thrown into a bucket, and the bucket's here.

There's a French paraffin teaching model from the 1800s, one of the best collections in the country of antique dental cabinets, the first electric drill, extraction keys from the late 1700s, an 1800s student chair with a cylindrical case for hot coals to warm the patient's feet (who said there were no conveniences in those days?), a wooden x-ray machine (that leaked), a toothbrush collection from the 1800s, a foot-operated pedal drill, and more artifacts from the profession.

Susan will recount the stories and histories behind the artifacts. She comes by her knowledge naturally; her father was a dean of the school. Guaranteed, you'll leave with a good taste in your mouth.

Mummers Museum

Address: 1100 South 2nd Street (zip 19147) (map page 119)
Phone: (215) 336-3050
Hours: Tuesday-Saturday 9:30 to 5, Sunday noon to 5 (closed Sunday July-August), Tuesday 9:30 to 9:30 May-September
Admission: adults $2.50, seniors and under 12 $2.00
Handicapped access: fully accessible
Parking: free lot on premises, metered and free but timed street parking nearby
Time needed: 1-1/2 hours
Location: SW corner of 2nd Street and Washington Avenue, about 1-1/2 miles south of Center City

Philadelphia's annual New Year's Day Mummers Parade has been a tradition in its present form for over a hundred years. It's a day-long festival stretching three miles along Broad Street (although in 1995 the parade followed Market Street for the first time). This museum commemorates the parade and all the preparation that goes into it.

There are four categories of marching units in the Mummers Parade: the Comics, Fancy Division, String Bands, and Fancy Brigades. Competition within each category is intense, with pride being sought more than the actual monetary value of the award.

As you enter the museum you'll see the "winner's circle" in the lobby, displaying the current year's winning costumes. There's also a 45-minute video showing highlights of the 1992 parade, which, if you've never seen the parade live or on local TV, will serve as a good introduction to the exhibits you'll see when you go to the main part of the museum on the second floor.

Once upstairs, go clockwise through the displays. You'll enter a large room with lifesize award-winning costumes and giant photos of the parade. The costumes, or "frame suits", weigh about 150 pounds, or more than many of the people wearing, or should we say, carrying, them. A display of the origins of "mummery" is in the next room, including large photos of marchers, and costumes. In the string band section, you can orchestrate your own version of "O, Dem Golden Slippers" by pushing buttons to hear various instruments playing their parts. That song is the parade's unofficial theme, having been part of the parade since it was

124

written in 1879 by Philadelphian James Bland. In real life, the string bands play other songs besides that one. In fact, in recent years the musical selections have become more varied and less march-like, as dance numbers have replaced the simpler practice of marching in formation and periodically stopping to play for the audience or judges.

If you can't attend a Mummers Parade or watch it on TV, the museum is the next best thing. There's a gift shop just inside the front door where you can buy parade souvenirs and memorabilia.

Mütter Museum

Address: 19 South 22nd Street (zip 19103) (map page 119)
Phone: (215) 563-3737
Hours: Tuesday-Friday 10 to 4
Admission: adults $2.00, seniors and students $1.00
Handicapped access: fully accessible via rear entrance; call in advance
Parking: metered street parking and public lots nearby; spaces may be limited
Time needed: about 1 hour
Location: SE corner of 22nd and Ludlow Streets, between Market and Chestnut. Subway (Market-Frankford line) to 22nd and Market, walk south 1/2 block.

This museum could easily go to your head, with its collection of skulls as well as other body parts. Owned by the College of Physicians of Philadelphia, this is not a medical school in the common usage of that term. It is, and has been since 1787, a place where physicians got together to share knowledge and discuss medical science's latest advancements. The Mütter Museum is named for Dr. Thomas Dent Mütter, who in 1858 started the display of pathological specimens as teaching tools for medical students.

Located in a beautifully paneled two-story room toward the rear of the College building, its main attractions include the skulls, skeletons, and replications of various pathologies. There are fractured skulls (which must have caused the death of the subjects on view, otherwise they probably wouldn't be here); a skeleton of a 7-foot-6-inch giant and a 3-foot-6 dwarf, both from the 1800s; fetal skeletons from the second month of gestation to post-partum; and perhaps the weirdest item in the collection, the "Soap Lady"—the x-ray of a woman of mid-1800s Philadelphia whose soft body tissues decomposed into a waxy soap-like substance. There's a plaster cast of the original "Siamese" twins Chang and Eng, who lived to adulthood and produced ten and eleven children, respectively.

Aside from its more ghoulish aspects, the museum is a wealth of medical history, with 1790s vintage American doctors' instruments, early electrocardiography equipment, and a 1953 full-scale replica of the first successful heart-lung machine. There are drawers of objects swallowed and inhaled by patients of Dr. Chevalier Jackson, a pioneer in bronchoesophagology. You name it, someone (intentionally or not) ate it, and the good doctor retrieved it. His laryngoscopes and bronchoscopes are also here.

There are cases upon cases of all sorts of medical instruments, from the common stethoscope to more exotic fare that you hope will never have to be used on you. Naturally, as befits its scientific setting, all items on display, whether instruments, diseased body parts, or skeletal remains, are identified as completely as the original documentation provided.

This is a fascinating museum, and even the squeamish have nothing to fear in making the rounds of the thousands of artifacts on view.

Neon Museum of Philadelphia
Address: 860 North 26th Street (zip 19130) (map page 119)
Phone: (215) 232-0478
Hours: anytime
Admission: free
Handicapped access: not applicable—see description below
Parking: may be limited at some locations—see below
Time needed: several hours for complete coverage
Location: numerous sites in Center City; get list at Davidson Neon Company, 860 N. 26th St. (SW corner of Poplar), about 4 blocks north of Philadelphia Museum of Art at Benjamin Franklin Pkwy. and Spring Garden St.)

The Neon Museum isn't really a museum in a sense that there's no one place you go to see the exhibits, and in another sense that the exhibits are part of the decor of other businesses around the city. As owner Len Davidson describes in his list of exhibit sites, "the museum's gallery space is the city itself".

Len, a sociologist by training, has always had a fascination for the colorful neon advertising signs that were a ubiquitous part of the urban American landscape from the 1930s through the 60s. In 1985 he started the museum to save, restore, and re-display these fast-fading relics. Over the years he's found new homes for his resurrected treasures and uses the "museum" to spread the word about them.

So the first stop on your Neon Museum tour is at Davidson Neon at 26th and Poplar in the Fairmount neighborhood, a few blocks north of the Art Museum. There you'll get a list of the currently visible signs and their locations. From there it's up to you as to which ones you check out. This is not a treasure hunt; the sites are all easy to find with a street map (you need only the map on page 119 if you're just going to the sites listed below), but you'll need several hours and a car or bicycle to get to all of them. You can take in quite a few as you travel between the other Center City sites described in this book. Most of these signs are visible from the street without going inside the businesses. The most centrally located signs are listed below, in a geographical sequence from east to west that minimizes backtracking.

Beauty Shop Silhouette—at Rockerhead, 619-A S. 3rd St., between South and Bainbridge Sts.
Animated Neon Fish—at CopaBanana, SE corner of 4th & South Sts.
Buster Brown and Tige—at Jim's Steaks, SW corner of 4th & South Sts.
Pontiac Indian—at American Diner, NE corner of 5th & Spring Garden Sts.
1930's Clock—at Down Home Diner, Reading Terminal Market, 12th & Arch Sts.
Chase Wheel Clock—at T.L.A. Video, 1808 Spring Garden St.
Simple Simon and the Pieman, and Pearl Beer Clock—at Down Home Grill, SW corner of 18th & Spring Garden Sts.
Mobilgas Pegasus and Bulova Watches Clock—at Diner on the Square, NE corner of 19th & Spruce Sts.

There are three others you can view a block away from Davidson Neon. They're the Lamplighter (formerly of Howard Johnson's fame), Petro Oil Burners Clock, and Poplar Street Face, a neon sculpture by Davidson using found objects. All are at the North Star Bar, 27th and Poplar.

Polish-American Cultural Center

Address: 308 Walnut Street (zip 19106) (map page 119)
Phone: (215) 922-1700
Hours: 10 to 4 on days open: weekdays January-April, Saturday added rest of year; closed holidays
Admission: free
Handicapped access: not accessible due to steps into building
Parking: metered street parking and public garages nearby
Time needed: about 1/2 hour
Location: south side of Walnut between 3rd and 4th. Subway (Market-Frankford line) to 5th & Market, walk south two blocks on 5th, left 1-1/2 blocks on Walnut.

This small museum honors via portraits some of the major Polish heroes—Tadeusz Kosciusko (general who served in American Revolutionary army), Adam Mickiewicz (national poet of Poland), Nicholaj Kopernik (Copernicus, father of modern astronomy), Frederic Chopin (composer), and Marie Curie (chemist, discoverer of radium). There are folk objects, such as costumes and decorative boxes, and coats of arms of Polish provinces or cities. There is also a changing exhibit, currently a photo montage of Poland during World War II.

While too small to present an in-depth view of all aspects of Polish culture, the museum makes a worthy start toward highlighting the country's contributions on the world.

Shoe Museum
Address: 8th and Race Streets (zip 19107) (map page 119)
Phone: (215) 625-5243
Hours: by appointment only Monday-Friday 10 to 4
Admission: free
Handicapped access: fully accessible
Parking: metered street parking and public lots and garages nearby
Time needed: 45 minutes to 1 hour
Location: SW corner of 8th and Race. Subway (Broad St. line) to Chinatown (8th St. between Race and Vine), walk south 1/2 block; or Market-Frankford line to Market East (8th & Market), walk north 2 blocks on 8th.

Put your best foot forward and hoof it on over to the Shoe Museum, located on the sixth floor of the Pennsylvania College of Podiatric Medicine. Since 1976, the College has displayed hundreds of shoes dating from 200 B.C. to the present. The hallways are lined with display cases, and this is the only drawback to the museum: it lacks a dedicated space where the exhibits can be set up in a more visitor-friendly fashion. But don't let this inconvenience keep you from viewing this unusual and broad collection.

Curator Barbara Williams conducts the tours and will regale you with stories behind all the exhibits. The roughly 250 shoes (a term used loosely, because some of the specimens look like anything but) represent about a third of the total collection. There are exhibits of First Ladies' shoes, 19th century hand made roller and ice skates, high-button shoes, bridal shoes, clogs and wooden shoes, men's, women's, and children's shoes from 1850 to the present, sports stars' shoes (for example, Reggie Jackson's from the 1977 World Series, in which he hit five home runs), entertainers' shoes (Sandy Duncan's green suede boots from "Peter Pan"), and miniature shoes.

There are unusual shoes—one 20 inches long for a patient with gigantism, 3-inch "lotus" slippers (for Chinese women whose feet were bound from childhood to keep them tiny, and in the process, misshapen and useless), 1890s dress shoes with heels so high (6-1/2 inches) that they will not stand alone, yet show considerable wear. The Augustus Wilson Shoe Collection, on extended loan from the Mütter Museum (see page 125), includes ancient and unusual footwear from around the world.

Legends about footware and its cultural influences are examined. For example, the word "sabotage" came from the French "sabots"—heavy wooden shoes that came in handy for destructive purposes. And it wasn't until the last half of the 19th century that right and left shoes were made; prior to that, pairs were made from a single mold or "last", which only roughly resembled the foot. That's why the old shoes in the collection aren't identifiable as to which foot they belong to.

If it's rare, unconventional, or belonged to someone famous, it's likely to be here at the Shoe Museum. Step right in.

Pittsburgh (Allegheny County)

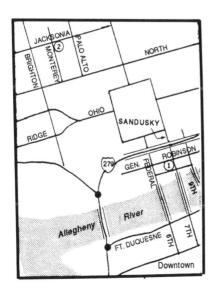

1 Andy Warhol Museum
2 Mattress Factory

Andy Warhol Museum

Address: 117 Sandusky Street (zip 15212) (map page 129)
Phone: (412) 237-8338
Hours: Wednesday, Saturday 11 to 6, Thursday-Friday, Sunday 11 to 8
Admission: adults $5.00, seniors $4.00, children over age 3 $3.00
Handicapped access: fully accessible
Parking: metered street parking and public lots nearby
Time needed: 1 to 1-1/2 hours
Location: just across Allegheny River from downtown in North Side neighborhood, at SW corner of Sandusky and Gen. Robinson Streets. Cross 7th St. Bridge onto Sandusky, continue 1 block to museum.

Think of this museum as a celebration of Andy Warhol, not as an art museum. Warhol was, in fact, much more than an artist.

The museum opened in May, 1994, in a former industrial warehouse built in 1911 just across the Allegheny River from downtown. It focuses on Andy Warhol the man, and all periods in his creative life. Warhol (originally Warhola) was born in Pittsburgh in 1928 to Eastern European immigrant parents. He's best known for his pop art, but he was also a filmmaker, magazine publisher, and portrait painter.

The 8-story building has been readapted to show Warhol's work in a setting similar to what he might have chosen himself. Ceilings were raised to allow for larger and more life-like displays. The spacious galleries have a simple, almost stark, appearance, which induces you to focus on the works on view rather than the surroundings. There are more than five hundred on display.

Exhibits are arranged by theme and period. These include his early commercial and consumer images of the 1950s and early 60s (the Campbell's soup cans Heinz boxes, and magazine advertisements), his famed 1960s portraits (Jackie Kennedy, Marilyn Monroe, and Liz Taylor), the more intimate and expressive portraits of the late 60s, and his more unconventional works such as "Rain Machine" and "Silver Clouds". His films and videos are shown on a changing schedule in the 6th floor film gallery.

The museum has about 900 paintings, 1,500 drawings, 77 sculptures, over 400 black-and-white photographs, and Warhol's wallpaper designs and books. The archives hold a complete set of Interview magazine, video and audio tapes, and scripts, as well as personal correspondence and diaries. The archival items will be available for public review as they are catalogued and preserved.

There is an entrance gallery, gift shop and coffee bar on the ground floor and a coffee shop in the basement, all with free admission during museum hours. Warhol, a man who used everyday life objects as his themes, would appreciate the "fifteen minutes of fame", and then some, that this museum brings him.

Mattress Factory

Address: 500 Sampsonia Street and 1414 Monterey Street (zip 15212) (map page 129)
Phone: (412) 231-3169
Hours: Tuesday-Saturday 10 to 5, Sunday 1 to 5
Admission: free
Handicapped access: fully accessible at Sampsonia, ground floor only at Monterey
Parking: free lot adjacent to Sampsonia, free but limited street parking nearby
Time needed: 1 to 2 hours
Location: about 1-1/2 miles north of downtown in Mexican War Streets section of North Side neighborhood. Sampsonia is eastbound alley between and parallel to Jacksonia Street and Taylor Avenue; 500 is 1/2 block east of Monterey Street. Monterey runs north for about 6 blocks from North Avenue; 1414 is at SE corner of Jacksonia. From downtown, cross Allegheny River via 6th Street Bridge onto Federal Street, circle halfway around Allegheny Center and continue north on Federal for about 4 blocks, then left on Jacksonia for about 4 blocks to parking lot on left opposite Garfield Street.

No, this is not a factory, and you won't see any mattresses, although they were made here in this building's earliest incarnation nearly a hundred years ago. This spot is best described as an alternative museum devoted to contemporary art, with emphasis on the contemporary. One of its unique characteristics is that some of the exhibits were built to be site-specific—designed for their location here and movable only at great effort and possible destruction of the work, and maybe the building as well.

Started in 1977 at the Sampsonia Street site, the museum expanded in 1988 to a former store and house around the corner at Monterey and Jacksonia. You would be hard-pressed to define a central theme for the place, other than its specialization in the unconventional.

Two examples that make that point: "Danaë" and "Pleiades", both by James Turrell. To view the former, get off the elevator on the third floor and turn left. Slowly proceed to your right around a darkened wall and turn left into a large room. Pause, then walk slowly toward a blue-grey rectangle. As for "Pleiades", start back at the elevator, turn left, then two rights, and enter a darkened doorway

131

to your left. Slowly walk up a ramp, being sure to hold the railings until you reach the end. Then sit in a chair on either side of you and look straight ahead for fifteen minutes. What will you see in these two images? I'm not going to spoil your fun by giving it away.

The artists whose works are here aren't household names, although some are well known within their gen*re*. The Mattress Factory is very willing, more than most art museums, to take a chance with the off-beat. To wit: after the Monterey street property was bought and a beat-up sink was found in a third-floor kitchen, curator Michael Olijnyk called British sculptor Bill Woodrow, who uses such relics in his work. He soon arrived and converted the kitchen into, not a disaster scene, but a scene of disaster. He poured gallons of gold paint onto the floor to simulate a room filling with water.

What more needs to be said about the types of exhibitions at the Mattress Factory?

Rodef Shalom Biblical Botanical Garden

Address: 4905 Fifth Avenue (zip 15213)
Phone: (412) 621-6566
Hours: June 1-September 15: Sunday-Thursday 10 to 2, Wednesday evening 7 to 9, Saturday noon to 1
Admission: free
Handicapped access: fully accessible
Parking: free lot in rear, free but timed street parking nearby
Time needed: 1/2 to 1 hour
Location: about 4 miles east of downtown in Oakland neighborhood, at NE corner of Fifth and Devonshire Street.

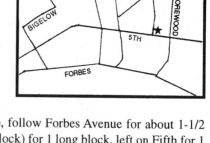

From downtown, take Penn-Lincoln Parkway (I-376) east to exit 6 (Oakland), follow Forbes Avenue for about 1-1/2 miles, left on Morewood Avenue (5000 block) for 1 long block, left on Fifth for 1 block to Devonshire.

This unusual garden is the only one in North America with ancient plants that all have Biblical references. There are over one hundred of these flora, all labeled with common and formal names, their normal habitat, and an appropriate Biblical verse.

The garden is the creation of Dr. Walter Jacob, Rodef Shalom's senior rabbi, and his wife Irene. They love plants, herbs, and gardens, and have written a book about the best of them, Gardens of North America and Hawaii (Timber Press). Irene conducts the tours if she's around; otherwise one of the trained (by her) docents will escort you. But if you want to hear the stories behind individual plants, as well as about the development of the garden itself, call ahead for an appointment so you get Irene's personal touch. On the first Wednesday of June, July, and August, you're invited to bring your lunch (the Temple provides cold drinks), enjoy it in the garden, and then take a guided tour. There's also a festival at the time of Sukkoth, the Jewish holiday celebrating the harvest. The date varies from late September or early October. These events fit the Jacobs' purpose in establishing the garden: bringing people closer to the Bible, and relating it to them in ways they most likely had not considered.

Not only are the plants true to the Holy Land, the garden itself is laid out in the same configuration as Israel, including the Jordan River, the desert, and En Gedi depicted by two bubbling springs. In Biblical times, plants had medicinal, nutritional, and religious uses. You'll see grains and fruit trees growing along with the herbs.

Having a Biblical garden located in Pittsburgh presents some problems, because Pittsburgh's climate is not like Israel's. Some plants that belong here bloom long before the garden opens for the season, others can't tolerate high humidity, and others can't survive a cold wet winter. So given a more favorable climate, there would be many more plants than there are, and the one-third acre wouldn't be nearly large enough to accommodate them.

While you're here enjoying the garden, don't neglect the Temple edifice itself. It's a National Historic Landmark, one of only five synagogues in the United States with that designation. It was built in 1907 and designed by Major Henry Hornbostel, the architect of Carnegie Mellon University a short distance away. The inspiration for the exterior came from a Turkish mosque in Constantinople.

Pottsville (Schuylkill County)

Jewish Museum of Eastern Pennsylvania
Address: 2300 Mahontongo Street (zip 17901)
Phone: (717) 622-5890
Hours: Tuesday-Thursday 10 to 3, Sunday by appointment
Admission: free; donation suggested

Handicapped access: fully accessible via basement entrance
Parking: free lot on premises
Time needed: about 1/2 hour
Location: west side of town; turn south off US 209 (Market Street) at 23rd, go 2 blocks to NW corner of 23rd and Mahontongo

There are other Jewish museums in the mid-Atlantic region, but what makes this one unusual is that a small synagogue with a declining membership has been able to put together the permanent and traveling collections it has.

The museum is in the lower level of Oheb Zedeck Synagogue, a congregation of about 65 families in a city of 16,000. Oheb Zedeck less than a generation ago had 200 families, when Pottsville's population was about 25,000. The synagogue has suffered the same fate over the past fifty years as the city, county, and anthracite coal region, as the loss of mining jobs and the other businesses they supported has not been offset by an increase in other skilled jobs.

The museum offers two traveling exhibits a year. When there is no loaned exhibit, they display their own collection. Recent offerings have included "Jews in American Cinema, 1898-Present", "Jewish Art and a Retrospective in Silver", and "Art in Israel". In 1996 there will be an exhibit on the life of Leonard Bernstein. If you're planning to visit, phone ahead to learn what's showing. Dolores Delin is the curator and one of the founders. Docents will guide you through the exhibits.

In addition to the exhibit on loan, the museum has displays that tell the story of the important Jewish holidays, the Sabbath, and the Torah reading ritual. There are historical records of this and other nearby congregations that no longer exist. The religious items on view all have explanatory labels, but some of the old photographs of the congregation's members have not yet been identified.

Another room contains a small chapel with the original pews, over 100 years old, from Oheb Zedeck's first synagogue. The chairs on the pulpit date from the 1700s. A tour to five remaining synagogues, all small, in towns such as Shenandoah, Mount Carmel, and Shamokin, can be arranged for those who are interested. Some artifacts from the now-closed Mahanoy City synagogue are here, and the stained glass memorial windows are from Reading.

This is not a "slick" museum, but if you view with the perspective of size and available resources, I think you'll be impressed by what this synagogue has accomplished.

Reading (Berks County)

The Pagoda

Address: Skyline Drive (mail to: Pagoda Skyline, Inc., P.O. Box 1615, zip 19603)

Phone: (610) 375-6399
Hours: daily 11 to 5; later closing in Daylight Saving Time
Admission: free
Handicapped access: not accessible due to steps from parking area
Parking: free spaces along road in front of Pagoda
Time needed: 1/2 hour

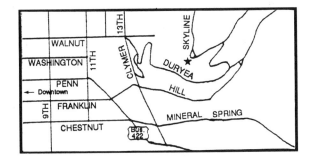

Location: east side of city atop Mount Penn. Follow Duryea Drive uphill through City Park for 1.5 miles from intersection of 13th and Walnut Streets. Road is not well signed; follow the uphill road at unmarked junctions.

This is the only Japanese Pagoda east of California, and has been here since 1908, when it was built as a resort at a cost of $50,000. But the 7-story structure never fulfilled its intended function, and within a few years was sold to the city for $1.00. It was restored in 1992 and now has a snack bar and gift shop. Standing 600 feet above the city, it affords a commanding view to the west and northwest, and to a lesser extent to the north and southwest. The gift shop is staffed by volunteers and is usually open Friday through Monday from noon to 4. All profits go toward maintenance of the Pagoda and surrounding area by Pagoda Skyline.

The Pagoda is 28 feet wide, 50 feet long, and 72 feet high. The walls are five feet thick at the base. Interior walls are concrete plaster, and the exterior walls above the first floor are frame, covered with red terra cotta tile shingles. Each of the five overhanging roof levels recedes two feet from the one below it. A total of 87 steps lead to the top of the building.

The bell in the observation room was cast in Japan in 1739 and was presented originally to *Shojenzi*, the Buddhist Temple at Yakuosan (now Tokyo).

The name "Duryea Drive" is historically important locally. Charles Duryea, the pioneer automaker, built his cars in Reading and tested them on the climb to the Pagoda. They reportedly made the grade in high gear.

Rome (Bradford County)

P.P. Bliss Gospel Songwriters Museum

Address: Main Street (mail to: RD 1, Box 293, zip 18837)
Phone: (717) 247-7683
Hours: Wednesday, Saturday 1 to 4 in summer, and by appointment
Admission: free; donations accepted
Handicapped access: accessible via rear door, but could be difficult inside due to
narrow doorways and placement of display cases
Parking: free in fire company lot across street
Time needed: about 1/2 hour
Location: west side of SR 187 in center of town, opposite fire hall; 7 miles north of
US 6 at Wysox

The Bliss Gospel Songwriters Museum is what this book is all about. Not
religious music, but unique places. The museum is here because some local citizens decided to preserve the memory, or perhaps more correctly stated, create an
awareness, of 19th century gospel songwriters, and so founded the museum in
1964.

Philip Paul Bliss was probably the most prolific songwriter, with 303
hymns and 541 published songs to his credit. Bliss and his wife were killed in a
train wreck in 1876; he was only 38, so he lost what might have been his most
productive years. He's memorialized in the museum's name because he and his
family lived for a short time in the house in which it's located, and most of the
items on exhibit pertain to him. The house is on the National Register of Historic
Places.

While most of the museum is devoted to Bliss, the lives and work three
other songwriters, Daniel B. Towner, Ira D. Sankey and James McGranahan, are
also commemorated. Towner was the only one of the four born in this area, but the
others found their way here (remember: "all roads lead to Rome.") and the community became a center for gospel music composition, with Bliss very much the
focal point. Towner was Bliss's pupil and later became the music department chairman at the Moody Bible Institute in Chicago, a post he held for 26 years until his
death.

136

As for the museum's contents, they cover the three rooms on the first floor and include sheet music, hymnals, personal possessions, Bliss's flute, and his melodeon, a small keyboard organ whose tones are produced by drawing air through metal reeds by foot-operated bellows. A few of Towner's articles are also on display. There is not a large collection of memorabilia, perhaps because nobody bothered to determine what existed, collect, and display it until 1964.

St. Michael (Cambria County)

Johnstown Flood National Memorial

Address: Lake Road (mail to: Box 355, zip 15951)
Phone: (814) 495-4643
Hours: daily 9 to 5 except Christmas; 6 PM close Memorial Day-Labor Day
Admission: free
Handicapped access: fully accessible
Parking: free lot on premises
Time needed: about 1 hour
Location: 10 miles NE of Johnstown via SR 56 and US 219. Take St. Michael-Sidman exit of US 219, follow SR 869 east for 1.3 miles to Lake Road, left for 1.6 miles to visitor center on right.

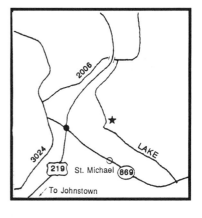

This site overlooks the former South Fork Dam whose failure unleashed the Johnstown Flood. The visitor center has a 35-minute movie about the flood and the events leading up it to; it's shown on the hour until one hour before closing. There are exhibits, artifacts, and models about the flood.

A one-mile round trip hiking trail leads to the site of the dam via the north abutment.

If you're planning to visit this Memorial, it should be in conjunction with a visit to the Johnstown Flood Museum (see page 102). Seeing both places will make your visit more meaningful, but coming here only is not especially worthwhile other than for the view of the Conemaugh valley and surrounding countryside you get from the visitor center or dam.

Scranton (Lackawanna County)

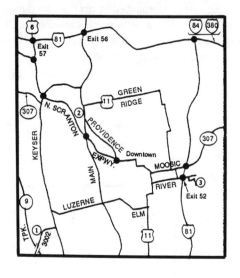

1 Anthracite Heritage Museum
  and Lackawanna Coal Mine Tour
2 Houdini Museum
3 Marine Corps League Museum

Anthracite Heritage Museum and Lackawanna Coal Mine Tour
Address: McDade Park, Bald Mountain Road (zip 18504)
Phone: (717) 963-4804 (Museum); 963-MINE (6463) (Mine Tour)
Hours: museum Monday-Saturday 9 to 5, Sunday noon to 5; mine tour April-November daily 11 to 4:30
Admission: museum—adults $3.50, seniors $2.50, age 6-17 $1.50; mine tour—age 12 and over $5.00, under 12 $3.50
Handicapped access: museum fully accessible; wheelchairs not recommended on mine tour
Parking: free lot on premises
Time needed: museum—about 45 minutes, mine tour—1 hour
Location: west side of city. Turn west (uphill) off Keyser Avenue (SR 3011) onto Bald Mountain Road (SR 3002) for 1/2 mile to entrance on right. From I-81, take exit 57, go south on US 11 for 1 mile to Keyser Avenue exit, then south on Keyser for 2.9 miles to SR 3002.

While Eckley Miners Village (page 92) focuses on the social aspects of the life of a coal miner and his family, the Heritage Museum and Mine Tour concentrate primarily on the working side. The Museum is operated by the Pennsylvania Historical and Museum Commission, while the Mine Tour is owned and operated by Lackawanna County.

138

The museum exhibits, as you'd expect, miners' tools and job-related equipment. There's also a "lifetime of work" exhibit and a saloon. Why a saloon, you ask? Saloons represented one of the first businesses an immigrant could form or work in, one where he made personal contacts that often led to other jobs. The saloon was perhaps the most important social setting in small mining towns, after the church, and it had nothing at all to do with alcoholism. For men, the bar was probably a more important meeting place than the church; if nothing else, they were in the saloon more often than in the church.

A miners' wash house has recently been added to the exhibits, as was a façade for a silk mill. Silk mills were also prevalent in northeastern Pennsylvania, although they developed after mining started to decline.

Several facets of immigration and ethnicity of the region have just been added and changed, such as a Catholic church altar, which has been set up as if in a church, not freestanding as it had been.

The Mine Tour takes you 300 feet below the surface into veins that crisscrossed under the city of Scranton. In fact, it was possible to enter the tunnel here and travel across the valley to East Mountain. The tour doesn't go quite that far, but you'll ride in an open car on a cog railway deep into the mine, where you'll step out and be guided on foot through part of the maze of tunnels. The guide will explain how the tunnels were dug, what safety precautions were taken, and how the coal was extracted. If you ever entertained any ideas about becoming a coal miner, this tour will bury those thoughts.

Bring a jacket or sweater for the tour, even on hot days, as the temperature in the mine is a damp 55 degrees.

Houdini Museum

Address: 1433 North Main Avenue (zip 18508)
Phone: (717) 342-8527 or -5555
Hours: daily by reservation only
Admission: adults $6.00, children $5.00
Handicapped access: one step to entrance, otherwise wheelchair accessible
Parking: free private lot in rear, free street parking nearby
Time needed: 2 hours
Location: in Providence neighborhood, on west side of Main Avenue (SR 3013) between Providence Road and Green Ridge Street. From I-81 exit 56, go south on Main Avenue for 2.0 miles to museum on right.

The Houdini Museum relocated to Scranton in 1986 after thirteen years in New York City. Why Scranton? Harry Houdini's wife's family lived here, so he spent a lot of time here as a visitor and performed often in this area.

The museum's main attraction is the multi-media show highlighting the legendary escape artist's feats. Because the time required for the full tour limits the number that can be offered per day, owner John Bravo asks visitors to make reservations.

You'll also see artifacts and props used by Houdini in his escapes as well as personal property that give an insight into his character. These displays change periodically, as there's only about one-tenth of the collection on view at any given time. There are demonstrations of a variety of tricks, and a magic show is being added in July and August. This is a great place to take the kids, who will be kept entertained constantly, so you don't need to worry that their attention will wane before the show ends.

The souvenir shop sells a variety of games, magic tricks, and related items that will let you impress your friends with your supernatural powers.

Marine Corps League Museum
Address: 1340 Alder Street (zip 18505) (map page 138)
Phone: (717) 347-USMC (8762)
Hours: Saturday-Sunday noon to 6
Admission: free; donations accepted
Handicapped access: not accessible due to steps to entrance
Parking: free lot on premises
Time needed: 30 to 45 minutes
Location: on East Mountain, about 1 block east of I-81. From 81 northbound, take exit 52, turn right at end of ramp onto River Street, go 1 block, right on Blucher Street for 1 block, left on Alder 1/2 block to museum. From 81 southbound, take exit 52 to Moosic Street, right 1 block to Meadow Avenue, left for 2 blocks to River Street, left across 81 and proceed as above.

This museum is another example of local initative and volunteer effort creating a worthy attraction. It opened in 1987 in a stone building built in the 1930s by the WPA as a neighborhood recreation center.

The museum contains six dioramas, all built by museum originator Jerry Maus, Sr., portraying the Marine Corps in wartime action from the Revolution to World War II. Other exhibits represent the Corps' history, from its founding at Tun

140

Tavern in Philadelphia to displays of present-day equipment. In between, there are Revolutionary and Civil War relics; a World War I uniform, helmet, mess kit, compass, gas mask, and canteen; a similar showcase of World War II effects; and one for the Vietnam War.

Other dioramas include one of Tarawa (this one was built by a Long Island Marine), the Guadalcanal airfield, Belleau Wood (one of the few Marine battles fought in Europe), and the Korean and Vietnam Wars. A gas-operated field kitchen has been set up.

Photos and drawings of Congressional Medal of Honor winners line the walls, and there are three display cases filled with air wing equipment. Rounding out the collection are authentic maps, charts, and other documents. The Marine Corps emblem has been carved into the floor. There's a video on the Corps' history that's shown in the basement social hall.

The museum is an industrious effort by the Northeastern Pennsylvania Detachment of the Marine Corps League, earning them a Distinguished Service award. Now if they could only get the city of Scranton to repave the street leading up to the museum. Perhaps they prefer to keep it in its mine-field state to create the proper mood for arriving visitors.

Shartlesville (Berks County)

Roadside America
Address: Old Route 22 (zip 19554)
Phone: (610) 488-6241
Hours: July-Labor Day: Monday-Friday 9 to 6:30, Saturday-Sunday 9 to 7; rest of year: Monday-Friday 10 to 5, Saturday-Sunday 10 to 6
Admission: adults $3.75, age 6-11 $1.25
Handicapped access: fully accessible
Parking: free lot on premises
Time needed: about 1/2 hour
Location: just west of town. From I-78/US 22 take Shartlesville exit to old 22, right for 1/2 mile to entrance on right.

For some sixty years, people have been pulling off US 22 to visit Roadside America, the Depression-era creation of Laurence Gieringer. Using his carpentry skills in his hobby of carving model buildings, he gradually expanded his repertoire to include carriages, bridges, and houses. Eventually he needed a place to display his work, and that's how Roadside America was born.

It has grown to include layouts of modern and Victorian villages, farms, grist mill, coal mine, and pastoral scenery, with model trains running throughout. The entire display is at a scale of 3/8 inch to the foot and has remained unchanged since Gieringer first built it, except for the addition of more up-to-date automobiles on the streets. There are no plans to alter anything else, according to Gieringer's daughter Alberta Bernecker, the present owner, because "we have to keep it the way Dad created it."

There's a gift shop on the premises where you can add to or start your own collection of model buildings, planes, cars, ships, and trains.

State College (Centre County)

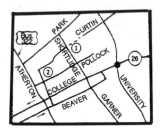

1 Frost Entomology Museum
2 National Cable TV Center

Frost Entomology Museum

Address: Head House III Building, Curtin Road, Penn State University (zip 16802)
Phone: (814) 863-2865
Hours: Monday-Friday 9:30 to 4:30 except holidays
Admission: free
Handicapped access: not wheelchair accessible due to step into building
Parking: non-reserved lots, metered street spaces, and garage scattered throughout campus; however, road access restrictions may limit convenience of some parking areas. Inquire at Pollock Road entrance to campus located on North Atherton Street (US Business 322).
Time needed: 30 to 45 minutes
Location: south side of Curtin Road between Shortlidge and Bigler Roads. Enter campus via Pollock Road (see above) or at College Avenue (SR 26) and Shortlidge Road.

This place will drive you buggy. The museum houses only about half a million specimens of insects and related arthropods representing about 10,000 species. The collection was started in 1937 by, and is named for, Dr. Stuart Ward Frost.

Most of the museum is viewable on your own, but the special collection rooms are open only with guides, so it pays to call in advance if you want to see it all.

While the major focus is on Pennsylvania insects, the collection is by no means limited to those. Dr. Frost himself added Florida insects to the museum and collections of others have been acquired over the years. There are displays of stinging insects of Pennsylvania, forest and desert dwellers, and glass aquariums housing insects that live in water. You'll also see an instructive exhibit on insect collecting and preservation. Yes, there are live displays as well, with honey bees, hissing cockroaches, and tarantulas. Most, but not all, specimens are identified.

The collection has outgrown its space, with display cases lining the hallway. A more appropriate setting for this excellent museum is in order.

National Cable TV Center
Address: Sparks Building, Penn State University (zip 16802)
Phone: (814) 865-1875
Hours: Monday-Friday 10 to 4 except holidays
Admission: free
Handicapped access: not accessible due to steps at entrance
Parking: non-reserved lots, metered street spaces, and garage scattered throughout campus; however, road access restrictions may limit convenience of some parking areas. Inquire at Pollock Road entrance to campus located on North Atherton Street (US Business 322).
Time needed: about 1/2 hour
Location: basement of Sparks Building, east side of Fraser Road between Pollock and Curtin Roads. Enter campus at Pollock Road and North Atherton Street (US Business 322).

The Cable TV Pioneers established this museum in 1989 as an educational and research center as well as a place to exhibit relics and artifacts from the cable industry. Cable TV had its more-or-less official birth in the late 1940s, building on technology then in use. Pamela Czapla, the director, will tune you in to all the gadgetry on display.

In the technical room you'll see the evolution of equipment used in the industry, as it would have appeared in your home. There are videos and other mementos of milestones in cable's development. Note the late 40s screen magnifier—remember the small rounded screens those early TVs had? Along with the gear from the stone age of electronics, you'll see the latest bells and whistles used by the industry today.

Admittedly, this is a place that the technological cognoscenti would enjoy most.

Titusville (Crawford County)

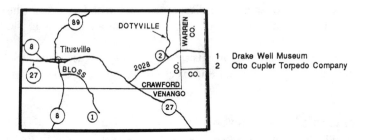

1 Drake Well Museum
2 Otto Cupler Torpedo Company

Drake Well Museum

Address: Bloss Street (mail to: RD 3, zip 16354)
Phone: (814) 827-2797
Hours: May-October: daily except Monday 9 to 4:45; November-April: Tuesday-Saturday 9 to 4:45, Sunday noon to 4:45; closed holidays except Memorial, Independence, and Labor Days
Admission: adults $4.00, seniors $3.00, age 6-17 $2.00
Handicapped access: fully accessible
Parking: free lot on premises
Time needed: 1 to 1-1/2 hours
Location: 1-1/2 miles SE of town. From center of town, take SR 8 south for 1/4 mile, left on Bloss Street (SR 2024) for 1-1/4 miles to museum. SR 2024 becomes SR 1011 at Venango County line.

This museum is owned by the Pennsylvania Historical and Museum Commission and commemorates the location where the world's first discovery of oil was made. It's not its historical significance that puts Drake Well in this book, but presence of the artifacts and structures that make the story complete.

144

Begin at the museum, where you can see a half-hour movie recounting the events leading to Drake's discovery. The movie is dated and stars Vincent Price as Drake, but more important, it's little more than an advertisement for its producer, the American Petroleum Institute. The museum's purpose is to set the stage for the kinds of events and actions that took place in the buildings outside, and still take place in others like them throughout northwestern Pennsylvania.

During the summer, you can travel about 10 miles southeast from Titusville to Pithole, now an oil ghost town preserved as a park. No buildings remain, but cellar excavations and street outlines are visible, and there's a visitor center. Take the walking tour using the printed guide which points out the locations of about sixty sites.

Inasmuch as the originals were built of wood and not designed to last forever, the outbuildings are all replicas. It wasn't financially sensible to erect durable buildings when they were expected to have a relatively short service life. As one oil well went dry, the rigs and other structures were abandoned and new ones built at another site. However, Drake's original successful hole is still there, now covered by a replica of his drilling rig.

Elsewhere on the grounds are the engine house, field office and oil lease exhibit (showing how more than one well could be pumped from a single power source), a transit pipeline station, and cyclone drilling rig. There is a gift shop in the former visitor center and several picnic areas on the property. The northern entrance to Oil Creek State Park, a 13-mile linear park extending south along the creek, adjoins the museum property, offering additional recreation opportunities.

Otto Cupler Torpedo Company

Address: Dotyville Road (mail to: P.O. Box 119, Pleasantville, PA 16341)
Phone: (814) 827-2921
Hours: Saturday-Sunday 3:30 from approximately second weekend in June to third weekend in October
Admission: adults $5.00, seniors $4.00, children under 18 $3.00
Handicapped access: ramp installed on grass surface between parking lot and seating area
Parking: free lot on premises
Time needed: special effects show: about 45 minutes; show and quonset hut tour: about 1-1/2 hours
Locations: Special effects show: 3 miles east of town. Take SR 27 east for 2.0 miles, left on SR 2028 (at sign "Pittsfield left 27 miles") for 1.1 miles, left on Dottyville Road (unpaved) for 1/2 mile. Quonset hut tour: same as above; hut is on

left side of SR 2028 just before Dottyville Road.

You'll get a bang out of this one. The Otto Cupler Torpedo Company, which is still in business, was founded in 1865 to produce explosives to enhance the yield of oil wells. They patented a process in which an explosive, usually nitroglycerin, was poured into a torpedo which was lowered into an oil well and then exploded, a process known as shooting. The force opened cracks in oil-bearing rocks, thereby increasing the well's production. Many otherwise marginal wells were made profitable in this manner.

But it was, of course, a dangerous way to make a living. For safety reasons, the nitroglycerin mixture was not concocted in towns, but rather in the nearby woods. Numerous shooters lost their lives in explosions. The Otto Cupler firm had its share of casualties, too, but has not had a fatal accident since 1937. In 1991 the company stopped using nitro.

Rick Tallini, Cupler's vice president, originated the idea of recreating the work of the shooters and in 1994 began presenting a 35-minute skit at a former nitro plant, well hidden in the woods as the originals were, where he set up a replica oil well, shooting platform, and bleachers for the spectators. This secluded site is also necessary to minimize the sound impact of the explosions, of which there are several during the course of each show. To go along with the skit, there's also a museum in a quonset hut about half a mile away where the tools of the trade are on view, as well as a movie about the shooting of Drake's well in Titusville.

The special effects show can fall victim to the weather, but even if cancelled, the museum remains open. Since this is a new endeavor, the programs are still evolving, as is the schedule, so it's best to call ahead.

If any place in this book is unique and unusual, it's this one.

Townville (Crawford County)

World of Mazes
Address: Box 33A, Mercer Road (zip 16360)
Phone: (814) 967-3307
Hours: May-September: Tuesday-Sunday and holiday Mondays 10 to 10; April, October: Saturday-Sunday 10 to 9
Admission: age 4 and over $2.50
Handicapped access: difficult due to gravel paths through maze

Parking: free lot on premises
Time needed: about 1/2 hour
Location: about 2 miles NW of town. Take
SR 408 for 1 mile west of town, turn right
(north) onto Mercer Road, go 1.7 miles to
entrance on right. Last 1.1 miles are unpaved.

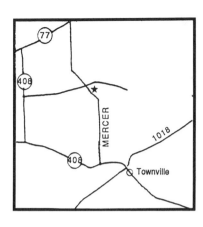

A-maze-ing! Chuck Himes is a
man who turned his hobby into a business,
and a very successful one at that. Long a
fan of mazes, he started creating them for
fun to while away junior high study halls.
Soon he had his classmates doing them.
Then came selling his puzzles to magazines, later he produced a book with his
creations, and in 1991 opened his first outdoor maze on his 17-acre property in
rural Crawford County. As of now there's only one 50-by-50 foot walk-through
maze, but construction of the world's largest maze (about 100-by-250, or over half
an acre) is on the horizon. Not far behind is a maze theme park. It'll all be right
here, unless the local government gives him problems. And after that, maybe a
chain of maze parks across the country. The business is still small enough that
Chuck and his business partner and wife Theresa can handle it themselves, but
they foresee the not-too-distant day when they'll have to hire help.

When you arrive you're given a clue card with the names of eight creatures inhabiting the "Magic Castle" (the maze). Your job is to find all eight and
write down their code numbers, then (if you find your way out of the maze) check
your answers in the gift shop. If you solved this maze and want to do more, there
are puzzles, games, and, yes, more of Chuck's mazes in book form.

Valley Forge (Chester County)

Freedoms Foundation at Valley Forge
Address: SR 23 (zip 19482)
Phone: (610) 933-8825
Hours: Monday-Friday 9 to 5
Admission: free
Handicapped access: fully accessible
Parking: free lot on premises
Time needed: 1/2 to 1 hour

Location: north side of SR 23, 1.0 miles west of SR 252, 3.4 miles west of entrance to Valley Forge National Historic Park

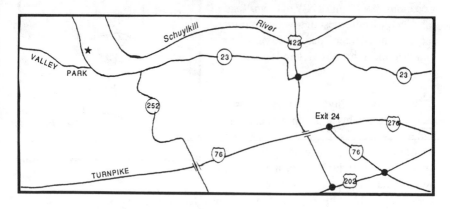

The Freedoms Foundation was founded in 1949 as a non-partisan, non-profit, privately funded organization dedicated to promoting responsible citizenship and teaching American history as it relates to our Constitutional freedoms. While most of the Foundation's work is outreach rather than a museum operation, there are indoor and outdoor displays of interest to visitors.

Most of the exhibits of public interest are outdoors on a 105-acre site. About half the acreage is devoted to the Medal of Honor Grove, with each state, the District of Columbia, and Puerto Rico represented on its own acre. The Grove is laid out in the shape of the U.S., with each state correctly positioned. The names of all Medal of Honor winners from each state are affixed to a 7-foot, 7-inch high obelisk, modeled after the Washington Monument, along with the state's seal and a dedication plaque; there are 52 obelisks, some stone, some fiberglass.

The Henry Knox Building, dedicated in 1966, houses archives and photos of many Medal of Honor winners. The other building open to visitors, Martha Washington, has flags from all fifty states and busts of the Foundation's founders. The Atrium of the building, with its "Independence Garden Floral Galeria", is used for organizational functions.

Washington (Washington County)

Pony Baseball International Headquarters
Address: 300 Clare Drive (zip 15301)

Phone: (412) 225-1060
Hours: Monday-Friday 9 to 4 except holidays
Admission: free
Handicapped access: first floor only fully accessible
Parking: free lot on premises
Time needed: 30 to 45 minutes
Location: just east of town on south side of I-70-79. Take

exit 8 (Beau St./SR 136). Eastbound, turn left at end of
exit ramp onto Clare Drive, go 0.3 miles. Westbound,
turn left on Beau St., cross 70-79, then left on Clare Drive for 0.4 miles.

Pony baseball's headquarters is in an A-frame house overlooking the Interstate. Although it's not set up as a museum, a staff member will escort you through the collections of memorabilia.

Pony baseball originated in Washington in 1951, using a diamond halfway between Little League and normal regulation size. It covers boys and girls in the five to eighteen age range, with developmental leagues with names such as Shetland, Pinto, Mustang, and Bronco. The leagues progress in two-year increments, making a total of seven covering the fourteen years between entry level and legal adulthood. Pony is a friendly competitor to the better known Little League, and has its own World Series here, on a field adjacent to the headquarters, during the second week in August. Pony baseball is a growing sport, and the headquarters has virtually outgrown its building. It has enough land on which to expand, but may not be able to do so here because its only access is via a residential street with fairly expensive homes.

The game mementos—bats, balls, gloves, uniforms, scorecards, programs, team photos—fill most of the rooms that aren't used for staff offices. There are boxes and boxes of more memorabilia, which there's no space to display, in the attic.

Just down the hill from the house is a small diamond made of bricks inscribed with players' names in whose honor they were purchased. The World Series playing field is just around the corner of the hill, in a municipal park.

Unless you know or knew someone who excelled in pony baseball, you probably wouldn't have occasion to visit the game's headquarters, particularly as it's not really set up as a museum as its more famous Little League counterpart (see the next entry). Still, this is a unique place, and that's why it's brought to your attention.

Williamsport (Lycoming County)

Little League Baseball Museum

Address: US 15 (mail to: P.O. Box 3485, zip 17701)
Phone: (717) 326-1921
Hours: Memorial Day-Labor Day: Monday-Saturday 9 to 7, Sunday noon to 7; 5 PM close rest of year, closed New Year's, Thanksgiving, Christmas
Admission: adults $4.00, seniors $2.00, age 5-13 $1.00, family $10.00 maximum
Handicapped access: fully accessible
Parking: free lot on premises
Time needed: about 1 hour
Location: north side of US 15, 1/2 mile east of SR 554 intersection, 1-1/2 miles south of downtown Williamsport

Officially named the Peter J. McGovern Little League Museum in honor of Little League's first president, it opened in 1982 in a two-level building overlooking the Susquehanna River and the city of Williamsport. Little League ball was born here in 1939, and the LL World Series is held in adjacent Lamade Stadium around the third week in August.

The lobby, which is a re-creation of Lamade Stadium, has flags hanging representing the more than seventy countries with LL programs, and an enormous (110 by 15 feet) photo mural taken during the 1982 Series.

Just outside the right field foul line is the Founders Room, with historic memorabilia and a video from Little League's earliest days to its 50th anniversary in 1989. The Mary McGovern Diamond Theater shows a rotating series of films about baseball.

The four basement galleries are oriented toward the kids. The "Play It Safe" Room has hands-on videos about the dangers of drug and alcohol abuse, a nutrition exhibit, and safety equipment players must wear. In "The Basics" room there are displays of gloves from the period 1910-1960 and the manufacturing of balls and aluminum and wooden bats, as well as an interactive quiz on the rules of the game. Next, in the "Play Ball" room, both kids and adults can practice batting and pitching, then watch a replay on video monitors. The "Showcase" room has changing displays that usually include effects from LL grads who are now in the majors, and there are commemorative bats from World Series winning teams.

Returning to the main floor, you'll pass the Hall of Excellence and Gallery of Achievement, recognizing current honored Little Leaguers, and finally reach the "World Series" room, where you can watch tapes of exciting moments in the annual August competition.

The museum is noteworthy for its excellent exhibits, many of which are hands-on. It's definitely a home run.

Willow Street (Lancaster County)

Institute for Scientific and Biblical Research

Address: 214 Willow Valley Lakes Drive (mail to: 3196 Thistle Drive, Lancaster, PA 17601)
Phone: (717) 285-7404
Hours: to be announced
Admission: free
Handicapped access: fully accessible
Parking: free lot on premises
Time needed: unknown
Location: just off Beaver Valley Pike (US 222/SR 741), 1/2 mile east of SR 272 intersection, 4 miles south of Lancaster.

The Institute for Scientific and Biblical Research, based in Lancaster, plans to establish a Creation Resource and Education Center on the site of a former antique car museum. It will be modeled after the only other such center in the nation, in San Diego.

The Institute's mission is to present the creationist theory of the development of Earth and Man. Its purpose is to counter the evolution theory which, in its view, has pervaded most public aspects of life but which is based on faulty science and an assault on God. Exhibits are planned to represent major events and periods in the development of earth and man and to show how their view of how these occurred can be supported through scientific as well as Biblical research.

They plan a museum that will include interactive displays, videos, and slides, science labs in which creation theories will be demonstrated, and a library and bookstore. The ante-diluvian, flood and ice age, and post-flood periods as delineated in the Bible will be the time-centered themes under which the exhibits will fall. As examples, the ante-diluvian area will include the creation of light, basic laws of science, and pre-flood geology. The flood-ice age epoch will be recreated with a scale model of Noah's ark and its inhabitants, fossils, and conti-

151

nental separation as described in the Book of Genesis. The post-flood era will show the origins of races and nations emanating from Babel, an analysis of scientific evidence of for a "young earth" theory, and presentations on contemporary problems such as population growth, energy, food supply, and the ozone layer.

It's the museum that's the focus of this entry. It was not my intention to make a statement for or against the Institute. The Creation Center—particularly the museum—is included because it fits the criteria for the book. Readers are free to draw their own conclusions.

York (York County)

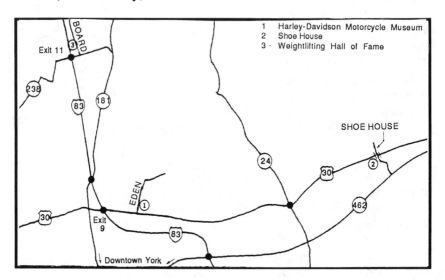

Harley-Davidson Motorcycle Museum
Address: 1425 Eden Road (zip 17402)
Phone: (717) 848-1177, (800) 673-2429, ext. HD
Hours: museum tours only: Monday-Friday 12:30, Saturday 10, 11, 1, 2; combined museum and plant tours: Monday-Friday 10 and 1:30. Closed holidays. No plant tours during annual model changeover closure late June-late July (museum open additional hours during changeover).
Admission: free
Handicapped access: fully accessible
Parking: free lot across street
Time needed: museum tour 1/2 hour, plant and museum tour 1-1/2 hours

Location: about 3 miles NE of downtown. From US 30, turn north at Eden Road traffic light, go 0.1 miles to parking lot on left. From I-83, take exit 9, go east on US 30 for 0.6 miles to left onto Eden Road (3rd traffic light).

Harley-Davidson is the only domestic motorcycle manufacturer, and this site is their only assembly plant (they make engines and a few other parts at plants in Wisconsin, but 70 percent of the bike is built here). The main reason for coming should be to tour the plant, as the museum is relatively small. Taken together, though, both can be an enjoyable hour and a half.

While waiting for the guided tour to start, you can watch a video on the company. Tours start in the museum, named for Rodney C. Gott, a former president of H-D. On view here are the company's bikes from its earliest in 1906 to current models. Not every year is represented, but the bikes on display show evolutionary changes in design, features, and construction techniques. The 1906 model had a belt-drive motor and cost $250. The earliest bikes were very similar to mopeds of today in size, power, and transmission.

During the 1920s and 30s, most of the company's production was police bikes, more powerful than they dared produce for public use. The cops needed the power to catch gangsters, whose cars could outrun normal police cruisers.

Some of the specialty bikes the firm has produced over the years include a 1958 Hollywood model bought by a number of movie stars, and bikes for wealthy industrialist Malcolm Forbes (he owned 60 of 'em). The Forbes bike exhibited here was around the world several times but only has 8,000 miles on it; he carried it to his destination in his own plane. In 1986 a Statue of Liberty commemorative bike was produced, and it's here as well. This one, and a mate, took a cross-country tour to raise funds for the Statue's restoration.

After the museum tour, you don safety glasses for the walk through the plant. Please note that children under 12 are not allowed on plant tours, and open-toed shoes and photography are also prohibited. (Cameras may be used in the museum, however.)

The plant tour includes the pre-painting polishing of metal parts, laser cutting of fenders and other parts from molds, tire mounting and wheel building, and the actual assembly line. There are three assembly lines here, one of which is for the sportster model. That line is different in that three assemblers build an entire bike rather than each working on a specific operation as the conveyor brings the parts to them. You'll also see new bikes being fueled and test-ridden for the first time. The testing is done indoors on rollers and takes about two minutes.

153

After the tour, when you return to the main building housing the museum, you're given a chance to look at the current models. But you can't buy, or even order, one on the spot; the company sells only through dealers. You can, however, buy souvenirs, such as H-D T-shirts, jackets, and caps in the small gift shop, and at least look the part while you wait from six to eighteen months for delivery of your new Harley.

Shoe House

Address: Shoe House Road (map page 152)
Phone: see below
Hours: daylight
Admission: not applicable
Handicapped access: fully accessible outdoors only
Parking: free lot on premises
Time needed: 5 minutes
Location: 5-1/2 miles east of downtown via SR 462 (East Market Street). Turn north onto Shoe House Road for 0.4 miles. From US 30 eastbound, take SR 24-Mount Zion Road exit, turn right on 24 south for 0.7 miles, then left on 462 for 1.9 miles to left on Shoe House Road. From US 30 westbound, take Hellam exit, turn left for 0.3 miles to 462, right for 0.9 miles to right on Shoe House Road.

The Shoe House, a local landmark since 1948, was closed at press time pending sale of the property. But you can still view it from the outside.

The house was built as an advertising gimmick by local shoe merchant Mahlon Haines. It's had several owners over the years, the most recent being Haines' granddaughter, who operated an ice cream stand and conducted tours of the interior.

For information on the house's current status, write the York County Convention and Visitors Bureau, P.O. Box 1229, York, PA 17405, or call (800) 673-2429, or (717) 848-4000 in the York area. Their visitor information centers are at 2958 Whiteford Road, just off US 30 at the SR 24-Mount Zion Road exit—open daily 9 to 5, or at 1 Market Way East downtown (NE corner of Continental Square, Market and George Streets)—open business hours on weekdays.

Weightlifting Hall of Fame

Address: 3300 Board Road (zip 17402) (map page 152)
Phone: (717) 767-6481

Hours: Monday-Friday 9 to 4:30, Saturday 9 to 3:30, closed holidays
Admission: free
Handicapped access: fully accessible
Parking: free lot on premises
Time needed: 30 to 45 minutes
Location: 5 miles north of downtown, just off I-83, exit 11. Southbound, turn left on SR 238 east, cross I-83, then first left onto Board Road for 0.2 miles to entrance on left. Northbound, cross SR 238 onto Board Road, go 0.2 miles to entrance on left.

The Weightlifting Hall of Fame is the creation of Bob Hoffman (no relation, although I knew him slightly), the founder of York Barbell Company, whose offices and sales facility are in the building. Bob was known as the "father of world weightlifting".

As you enter the lobby, you'll see a 40-foot crescent-shaped mural painted in 1959 by California artist Eric Askew, titled "Twelve Labors of Hercules". That pretty much sums up what the museum is all about.

The Hall of Fame consists of four parts: powerlifting, "strongmanism", bodybuilding, and weightlifting. Powerlifting differs from weightlifting in that it stresses brute strength, while the latter puts greater emphasis on technique. Powerlifting was accepted by the Amateur Athletic Union in 1965. The first national open tournament and first world championships were held in York, in 1964 and 1971, respectively.

Each segment of the museum includes photos of masters of the techniques, trophies of Olympic champions, posters of major events in the sports, stories about the competitors, and records.

Bob Hoffman made sure his own accomplishments were not overlooked; one wall is devoted to a biographical sketch and a display of his trophies, awards, letters of congratulations, and some of his collection of more than 600 replicas of bears. Starting in the 1930s, he was the publisher of "Strength and Health" magazine.

There was originally a Softball Hall of Fame here as well, as that sport became a passion with Hoffman later in life. However, that exhibit has been removed and is in search of a new home.

157

THE NATIONAL APPLE MUSEUM

Cut and Thrust
Edged Weapons

And Gallery Of Sporting Art

SPRING GARDEN PUBLICATIONS CO.

The Watch & Clock Museum of the NAWCC

514 Poplar Street
Columbia, PA 17512
717-684-8261

SPRING GARDEN PUBLICATIONS CO.

ORDER FORM

_____ GOING DUTCH: A Visitor's Guide to the Pennsylvania
Dutch Country @ $12.95   _____

_____ UNIQUE and UNUSUAL PLACES in the
MID-ATLANTIC REGION @ $9.95   _____

THE NEW YORK BICYCLE TOURING GUIDE
_____ Route ST (Southern Tier) @ $3.50   _____
_____ Route EM (Erie-Mohawk) @ $2.95   _____
_____ Route HC (Hudson-Champlain) @ $2.95   _____
_____ Route PC (Penn-Can) @ $2.50   _____
_____ Set(s) of All 4 Routes @ $9.95   _____

TOTAL FOR MERCHANDISE   _____

SHIPPING AND HANDLING:
BOOKS: $2.50 for the first book and $1.00 for each
additional book.   _____
BICYCLE TOURING GUIDES: $1.50 for one or two
Routes, $2.00 for three or four Routes, $2.50 for more
than four Routes. $1.00 if ordering Bicycle Touring
Guide(s) and books.   _____

OPTIONAL FIRST CLASS MAIL add $2.00   _____

SHIPMENT OUTSIDE USA add $2.00   _____

TOTAL DUE   _____

_ _ _ _ _ _ _ _ _ DETACH HERE _ _ _ _ _ _ _ _ _ _ _

Send check or money order (U.S. funds only, please) to Spring Garden Publications Co., PO Box 7131-B, Lancaster, PA 17604-7131.

OUR UNCONDITIONAL GUARANTEE: Examine any of our publications for ten
days. Then, if for any reason you're not satisfied, return them undamaged for a full
refund (excluding shipping charges). No questions asked!